> The Vegetarian Society's  someone who eats no meat
> or crustacea and also avoids
> terhouse such as gelatine, .
>
> vegetarians eat dairy food and free-range eggs.

" Cook with love and you will taste it in the food. " —John

"My then 9 year old daughter, Tamsin, had a long history of Acidosis, (an inability to break down fats in the liver), before we arrived at Findhorn. She was unable to eat things like crisps, french fries, ice cream or chocolate without becoming very ill. This was particularly difficult for her when going to children's parties, and we had to constantly be careful of what she ate. Some weeks after arriving at Findhorn and eating a vegetarian diet for the first time in her life, I realised that Tamsin could now eat everything and anything. She never had another episode of acidosis in her life." —Karin

"I remember that in Spain about 30 years ago I was overweight, lethargic and generally in bad shape health-wise. Then I switched to a strict vegetarian diet. Over 6–9 months, I shed 60 lbs and recovered my energy." —Tony

"I will never forget my introduction to Findhorn's delicious and abundant food. Peter Caddy's delicious cheese and mushroom omelettes were memorable. I think one of the reasons we like the food at Findhorn is that it is lovingly cooked for us by loving friends. Findhorn's cooks were light years ahead of today's gourmet chefs in the use of culinary herbs and edible flowers tossed into fresh garden salads." —Carly

"My copy of the Findhorn Family Cookbook *looks like all much loved cookbooks, ragged and dogeared. I've been using it regularly for the past 20 years and still discover new culinary surprises. Aside from one infidelity committed years ago with an irresistible Dutch smoked sausage, I keep to a vegetarian diet because I feel healthier on it, and because I love animals and am glad not to add to their suffering."* —Sarah

"I was suffering from several degenerative diseases and heading down a path of taking medications for the rest of my life, which I didn't want to do. I switched to vegan and within a week I felt like a new person. I had lots of energy, a positive outlook, moved better, reversed the degenerative diseases, and gradually went off the medication. That's what healthy food can do for you!"
—Shari

"Eating vegetarian just makes me feel better.... and LIGHTER!!! I am sure that it has something to do with the food chain and it not being so complicated. Most animals eat vegetables or grains to "fatten up". I like to by-pass the animal and go straight to the source—the vegetable! Oh yes, and I loved cooking really loving meals at Findhorn, that was the "secret" ingredient in all my meals: LOVE." —Loren

"At Findhorn, I was a complete vegetarian and enjoyed very good health, never had a cold in three years and always felt fit. Being a vegetarian also makes me feel more peaceful, and meditation is easier. I feel good living simply and lower in the food chain—easy to look a cow in the face. As a vegetarian your sweat doesn't smell bad and your breath can be better. I don't find that I have to depend on quick fixes of sugar and caffeine, and my energy level is steady. I can stay up late, get up early, and out walk many teenagers." —Helen (ageless!)

"For personal health reasons, I recently began eating only freshly juiced fruits and vegetables, organic salad greens, and a broad selection of grains and nuts. Not only have I lost almost fifteen pounds without even trying, I feel much healthier, have more energy, and have almost completely lost my craving for sweets. One of the remarkable things that I'm noticing is that due to the high nutritional value of what I'm eating, I can eat a whole lot less, and still feel satisfied. Now every day seems like a new adventure in feeding my body food that it really appreciates." —Sandy

"I eat vegetarian because it has evolved way beyond a load of old lentils and, as this cookbook shows, has developed into a truly haute cuisine. So even the most exacting hedonist can eat pure, clean and exciting!' —Amanda

тhe
flNDhORN
book of

Vegetarian Recipes

by
Kay Lynne Sherman

illustrated by
Sarah Zoutewelle Morris

this is an abriged and revised edition of a book previously published under the title
The Findhorn Family Cookbook:
a vegetarian cookbook which celebrates the wholeness of life
by Findhorn Press in 1981
This new, revised edition first published by Findhorn Press 2003

ISBN 1 84409 015 9

British Library Cataloguing-in-Publication Data.
A catalogue record for this book is available from the British Library.

Edited by Findhorn Press
Cover by Thierry Bogliolo
Internal book design by Karin Bogliolo
Calligraphy and illustrations © Sarah Zoutewelle Morris 1981, 2003
Cover background photograph by Digital Vision
Cover central photograph © Stockbyte

Printed and bound by WS Bookwell, Finland

Published by

Findhorn Press

305a The Park, Findhorn
Forres IV36 3TE
Scotland, UK

tel 01309 690582
fax 01309 690036
e-mail: info@findhornpress.com

findhornpress.com

Table of Contents

To Eileen and Joannie,
the original Findhorn cooks.
They have inspired us all

FOREWORD

When I arrived at the Findhorn Community in 1975 I had dabbled in vegetarianism, mostly because my new partner was vegetarian, and he seemed to look pretty good on it. He was also on what is often called "the spiritual path" and eating vegetarian food seemed to be part of this journey. However, I had found vegetarian cooking rather limited.

My first meal at Findhorn was a revelation. Lunch was a smorgasbord of dozens of different dishes, beans, grains, salads of every description, cooked vegetables, and delicious home-baked bread. There were also cheeses, jars of peanut butter and honey, and fruit. I have always enjoyed my food, particularly vegetables and salads, and I was in heaven!

Before I could say "adzuki beans" I found myself working in the kitchen, learning to cook for the first time in my life. However, before I was allowed to touch any of the ingredients I had to learn that one of the most important things when preparing food is to do so with respect and gratitude. Before any activity at Findhorn, groups attune to one another. In the kitchens, the group of cooks attune to each other and also to the beings overlighting the food, as well as the equipment and the space where they will be working. What is also important is to invoke and fill the meal being prepared with love and light, so that the people eating it will be nourished on all levels. Mostly my friends and I also invoked fun and laughter, which definitely seemed to "lighten" the food we made.

I loved my years in the kitchen, I learned so much more than just cooking. I discovered that preparing meals for my community was a creative and very satisfying activity. I also loved to see those happy, hungry faces arriving at meal times and to know that I had been able to serve my friends and family. I became not only more conscious of how I was cooking the meals, but also how I was eating the food. Knowing how much care and love went into the preparation meant that eating it with awareness and gratitude was just as important.

It's many years since I worked in the Findhorn kitchens. However, last year I was there doing some research for my book *In Search of the Magic of Findhorn*, and one of the important places where I looked for the "magic" was of course the kitchen! Yes, I found it was still there. New faces in the kitchen, even a new kitchen and new equipment (although I was happy to see the same Hobart mixer I used to make my famous Cheese Soufflé many years ago), but still the same enthusiasm, the same love and caring went into the food they were cooking. Forty years of vegetarian food has been prepared in the Findhorn kitchens, first by Eileen Caddy and Joanie Hartnell-Beavis, then by many hundreds of cooks who have put their energy and love into the food that has fed the ever-growing incredible family at Findhorn.

The recipes in this book are just a few of the meals we have all enjoyed over the years. It is also good to know that just as much love and care has gone into putting this book together, first by the group who wrote, illustrated and typeset the original version in 1981, and then again those of us who have been part of this new edition. When you prepare the recipes from this book, I hope you will experience the love and joy that is being beamed to you by Findhorn cooks past and present, and by one very happy publisher (and cook!).

Karin Bogliolo
Publisher, Findhorn Press

Necessary Information for Using this Book

Measuring:

The recipes are presented in metric, Imperial and American measurements. In the case of Imperial measurements, it has been more exact to use fluid ounce measures than pints in many cases, so it will be necessary to have a measuring jug which measures fluid ounces. As all measurements are standard, please use measuring spoons, cups and scales rather than guessing. All tablespoon and teaspoon measurements are meant to be level measures. *American teaspoons, tablespoons, cups and pints are a different size to British ones*, so if you look across the page and notice a different amount, that is the reason.

Ingredients:

Herbs – all herbs are dried, rather than fresh, unless specified otherwise.

Milk Powder – non-instant milk powder has been used in these recipes.

Miso – fermented soya bean paste used as soup broth base and as seasoning. Available in many different flavours from wholefood shops. Any of the flavours will do in these recipes.

Tamari – a natural soya sauce of very good quality, usually available in wholefood shops.

Tofu – soya bean curd.

Welcome

One of the many enjoyable aspects of a visit to the Findhorn Community is its vegetarian cuisine. After savouring a meal or working in the kitchens, guests have asked again and again, "How did you do it? May I have the recipe?" To all of our friends around the world who have wanted to bring a small part of the Findhorn Community into their own kitchens, we offer this book.

The cooks of the community opened their notebooks, kitchens and hearts to this creation. "Mary makes the best sherry trifles," someone told me one day, and the next thing I knew I was standing on Mary's front steps, cautiously asking if she'd be willing to offer her secrets for the cookbook. There was no hesitation. Mary was delighted to share the recipe. She graciously invited me for tea that lasted 'till suppertime and loaned me her hand-written notebook of favourites.

Thanks to many such responses, we present to you our everyday fare as well as our all-out festival splurges. For the pure and healthy, there's Peasant's Pie and Hearty Bean Soup. And for the unabashed sweetie-lovers, the tea party and desserts chapters will bring supreme satisfaction. (The recipe for Isla's cake alone makes owning the book worthwhile!)

At the Findhorn Foundation, the attitude of the cooks has a tremendous effect on the whole community; the same is certainly true in every home. The consciousness we bring to cooking is transferred to the food, and from there to our families. Cooking is really a way of giving to our loved ones, a daily ritual of attuning with the nature kingdoms who provide our fare, and with each other.

What we wish to share with you is that the most important ingredient in any meal is the love with which it is prepared. Love has the ability to lift and transform every meal and every situation. When we bring a spirit of attunement to our daily tasks, all we do is filled with love.

Kay Lynne

Cooks and Their Environment

The physical environment we cook in is important, and creating a kitchen that is light and loving can be a joyful task. At the beginning of each work shift in the Findhorn Foundation kitchens we stand in silence together, holding hands in a circle. In this way we align ourselves with each other, with the beings that guide us, and with the task at hand.

In your own home you can do the same: meditate in your kitchen or spend some quiet undisturbed time before starting to work. Notice what parts of the kitchen need attention: clean and paint; get rid of stale food; organize things; put the herbs in alphabetical order; buy some plants; invite a friend over for tea; ask the angels in.

It is a pleasure to walk into a kitchen where the equipment is well used and well loved. In our community kitchens we consider each tool to be a friend helping us to do a job. Most of our appliances have names and personalities and that adds an element of warmth to our tasks. Caring for our tools as they deserve adds to their longevity and makes our cooking job a more conscious one.

Wooden beings (spoons, cutting boards) are protected from soapy water and strong flavours, as they absorb everything. Wash them immediately after use; dry and put away. Don't leave the spoon to cook in the soup; it doesn't do the soup or the spoon any good. The wooden handles on knives deteriorate if they are left to soak, and the knife blade is dulled when it hits against other things in soapy water. So wash the knife immediately after use and put it away. Wooden boards may be lightly oiled if they become dry.

Metal beings (frying pans, woks, saucepans) should not be left to soak in water if they are made of iron, as it too absorbs flavours and tends to rust. If iron pans are treated well, they will need only a quick wiping out after use. If they do need cleaning, follow the method described for the omelette pan in the omelette recipe. If pans become dried out, season them with oil: slowly heat oil in the pan for 20 minutes, then pour it out and wipe the pan clean. Woks should be washed with water only and a stiff brush, immediately after use.

When buying kitchen equipment, be sure to keep in mind the people who will be using the kitchen. If children like to help, it's good to have some tools that are safe enough for them. If the kitchen is used by a large number of people, it is preferable to have simple indestructible equipment rather than sophisticated gadgets. In general, quality is preferred to quantity in kitchen equipment: better to have one very good knife than a whole set of mediocre ones. When Peter Caddy ordered the equipment for the original community kitchen, he drew from his experience as a catering officer in the R.A.F., and chose the best quality available, knowing the extensive use the kitchen would receive; over the years we have been grateful for his foresight.

The energy invested in your kitchen and in the tools you use will reap the rewards of efficiency and pleasure in cooking. So choose your utensils well, care for them as friends, and allow your kitchen to shine with Spirit.

Soups

*We are seeking to nourish your consciousness
to move into Oneness.
This does not mean that you ignore
the wisdom of a proper diet,
but that you include the most important
ingredients which are
awareness and love.*

*—David Spangler, 12 August 1971,
transmission on kitchen and food*

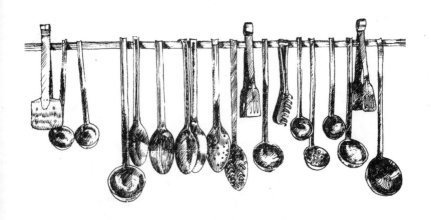

Soups can speak of warmth, of sharing, of nourishment.

The child arrives home and smells the aroma of the slowly simmering soup. Grandmother stirs the pot while listening to an account of the day. This scene is enacted again and again, with different people playing the parts, in different places and in different circumstances.

Stirring a pot of soup in one of the kitchens at Findhorn, the cook listens to the tale of woe or the tale of joy and again re-enacts the scene. In your kitchen, perhaps you hear a story from a loved one who needs understanding and nourishment. Soup is offered. The scene plays again.

Soups are nourishing; they are satisfying. Soups also vary greatly. They can be the simple first course, meant to prepare the palate for other tastes to come, or they can serve as the entire meal: Complex and hearty.

Soups can be an expression of creativity; recipes are the starting point, the inspiration. In this chapter there are recipes for soup, and there are suggestions about varying the recipes. There are also ideas for adding garnishes and other flavourings. Using these suggestions as a starting point for experimentation, you can vary the final result considerably. An ever-changing kaleidoscope, no two soups are ever the same.

As an example, after mastering the Hearty Bean Soup, try using different beans or several beans together. Try adding some of the ingredients mentioned in the section called "Making a Better Soup." Then try the same sort of variations using Grandmother's Vegetable Barley Soup as a starting point.

And remember to invite your loved ones into the kitchen. In that way the most important ingredient can be added to the soup: Your caring.

Stocks

Using vegetable stock as a base for soups really does make a difference!
Here are some relatively effortless ways to make vegetable stock.

Method No.1

Save the bits and pieces that are usually discarded from vegetables. Often the peelings and the most flavourful parts of carrots, greens, celery, cabbage, cauliflower, etc. get thrown away. Mushroom bits, onion skins and potato peelings are particularly valuable for their colour and flavour. As you are preparing a meal save those bits. Put them in a saucepan, cover them with cold water and let simmer gently on the back of the stove for at least 20 minutes. Turn off the heat, and let sit until cool. Pour through a strainer into a jar and keep in the refrigerator until you need it, or use immediately.

Method No.2

Save your vegetable cooking water. Keep it in a jar in the refrigerator until soup-making time. Caution: Don't add hot stock to the cold, as this seems to spoil it; rather, let the stock cool down first. Cooking water from any vegetable may be used, with the exception of beetroot, which gives a strong colour to the broth.

Method No.3

For those times when you are caught without stock, have a commercial substitute on hand. Miso or tamari can be added to soup to give it flavour, as can yeast extract, Marmite (British) or powdered vegetable broth. These, however, are emergency items only!

Making a Better Soup

*The most important rule is **taste the soup**.*
If you find it lacking, here are some suggestions:

To give it body, flavour and zip, add one or more of the following:

salt
miso
vegetable stock powder
tamari
Marmite
yeast extract
sautéed onions
sautéed celery leaves
Spices:
  coriander, cumin, cloves

Herbs:
  basil, marjoram, lovage,
  thyme, bay, parsley, celery,
  oregano
butter
milk or cream
lemon juice
garlic
left-over sauce or gravy

To thicken it, follow one of these methods:

1. Mix a bit of flour, arrowroot or cornflour (cornstarch) with cold water, and add to the soup.
2. Make a roux of butter and flour; after cooking for 5 minutes, whisk into soup.
3. Blend a portion of the soup.
4. Blend left-over spaghetti with water and add to soup.

To make the soup look appealing, use one or more of the following as a topping:

parsley
grated cheese
spring onions
chopped croûtons
chives, finely chopped
slivered avocado

chopped cucumber
any colourful vegetable, slivered very thin
paprika
nutmeg
gomasio
roasted nuts or seeds

Grandmother's Vegetable Barley Soup

1. Chop Onion, celery and leaves; then fry them in oil, in a large soup pot.
2. When vegetables are tender and beginning to brown, add water. Bring to a boil.
3. Rinse barley under running water, then add to boiling soup stock. Add bay leaf and simmer until barley is tender, about one hour.
4. Chop potatoes, carrots and tomatoes.
5. Add potatoes, carrots, tomatoes and tomato juice to soup; simmer until vegetables are completely done and beginning to get mushy, about an hour. If water boils away, add more.
6. Add green vegetables and basil at the last. Cook until vegetables are just tender.
7. Taste, and add salt if necessary.

Serving Suggestion

This is a hearty soup, which needs only a salad and homemade bread
to complete the meal. Serve topped with chopped parsley or grated cheese.

Variation: Italian Minestrone

1. Use olive oil to fry onions and celery
2. In place of barley, cook the equal amount of kidney beans and 1 tsp sage.
3. At the end, with the green vegetables and basil, add 110g/4oz noodles
and 1 tsp oregano. Cook until noodles are tender.

metric/imperial (10–12 servings)	american (10–12 servings)
1 onion	1 onion
inner stalks of a head of celery	inner stalks of a head of celery
2 Tbsp oil	2 Tbsp oil
2¼ litres/4 pints water	2½ quarts water
170g/6oz barley	1 cup barley
1 bay leaf	1 bay leaf
2 medium potatoes	2 medium potatoes
2 carrots	2 carrots
860g/1lb 14oz tin tomatoes	1lb 14oz tin tomatoes
225g/8oz green vegetable in season (e.g. courgettes or green beans)	1½ cups green vegetable in season (e.g. zucchini or green beans)
1 tsp basil	1 tsp basil
1 Tbsp salt	1 Tbsp salt

Potato Mushroom Soup

1. Wash and chop potatoes. In a soup pot, cook potatoes in boiling water or stock until almost soft.
2. Wash and chop vegetables. Sauté in 1 Tbsp butter until almost tender.
3. Brush or wipe mushrooms clean; slice and set aside.
4. In a small pan, melt butter; mix in flour and salt with a whisk. Cook over moderate heat for 5 minutes, stirring constantly, Whisk mixture into potato broth.
5. Add mushrooms and sautéed vegetables to potatoes and broth. Simmer for 25 minutes, stirring occasionally.
6. Just before serving, add crushed garlic and marjoram. Do not boil any more after that.
7. Serve topped with parsley.

Variations
- Instead of marjoram, add pepper and paprika, or dill, or chives.
Top soup with grated cheese.

metric/imperial (6 servings)	american (6 servings)
500g/18oz potatoes	3 cups chopped potatoes
1½litres/2¾ pints water or stock	7 cups water or stock
100g/3½oz mixed vegetables (such as cabbage, celery, carrots, cauliflower, tomato)	1 cup mixed vegetables (such as cabbage, celery, carrots, cauliflower, tomato)
1 Tbsp butter	1 Tbsp butter
100g/3½oz mushrooms	2 cups sliced mushrooms
55g/2oz flour	¼ cup flour
15g/½oz salt	2½ tsp salt
1 clove garlic	1 clove garlic
1 tsp marjoram	1 tsp marjoram
parsley	parsley

Loren's Onion Soup

1. Peel Onions; slice in thin crescents. (See vegetable chapter for instructions for slicing vegetables.)
2. Wash carrot and slice in matchsticks.
3. Fry fresh ginger and garlic in oil or butter. Add onions and carrots and fry lightly. As soon as vegetables are heated throughout, turn heat very low and continue cooking slowly, stirring occasionally, until onions are limp and completely tender (at least 30 minutes). If they have been cooked slowly enough, they will taste sweet.
4. Add stock and simmer for another 30 minutes.
5. Before serving, check the flavouring and add tamari or miso if needed for saltiness.

Variations

Add other vegetables, such as cauliflower or finely chopped kale. For French onion soup, omit the carrots. Top each bowl with croûtons, or with a round piece of toast. Sprinkle parmesan cheese on top and brown under the grill (broiler).

metric/imperials (4–6 servings)

680g/1½lb onions
1 medium carrot
1 tsp fresh grated ginger root
2 cloves garlic, minced
4–6 Tbsp butter or oil
1¼ litres/2 pints vegetable stock or water
tamari or miso to taste

american (4–6 servings)

8 cups onions
1 medium carrot
1 tsp fresh grated ginger root
2 cloves garlic, minced
4–6 Tbsp butter or oil
5 cups vegetable stock or water
tamari or miso to taste

The Simplest Soup

1. Wash and chop vegetables.
2. In a saucepan cover vegetables with stock. Bring to a boil, then simmer until tender.
3. Spoon vegetables, stock and a lump of butter into blender. Process until completely smooth.
4. Return to saucepan and heat to just under boiling point. Add water if needed and check to see if salt needs to be added.
5. Before serving add a bit of milk – just enough to make the soup turn a lighter colour. **Do not allow to boil after adding milk!**

metric/imperial

a fresh vegetable in season
a slice of onion and a few celery leaves
good vegetable stock
butter
salt
milk

american

a fresh vegetable in season
a slice of onion and a few celery leaves
good vegetable stock
butter
salt
milk

Suggestion

This is a good way to use little bits of leftover vegetables. Just heat them with their cooking water, then follow steps 3–5.

Cream of Tomato Soup

A refreshing first course

1. Hold tomatoes with a fork over heat until skin blisters. Immerse in cold water. Peel.
2. Heat milk in a saucepan.
3. In a blender, blend all ingredients except milk, until smooth.
4. With blender running, slowly and carefully pour in hot milk.
5. Return mixture to saucepan and heat to serving temperature. ***Do not allow to boil!***
6. Serve immediately.

metric/imperial (4 servings)

570ml/1 pint milk
450g/1lb very red, ripe tomatoes
30g/1oz butter
2 Tbsp flour
1 tsp salt
1 tsp honey
1 thin slice onion
1 sliver of garlic

american (4 servings)

2 cups milk
2½ cups very red, ripe tomatoes
2 Tbsp butter
2 Tbsp flour
1 tsp salt
1 tsp honey
1 thin slice onion
1 sliver of garlic

Suggestion

Most of the preparation for this soup can be done in advance: have all ingredients ready in the blender and milk in a saucepan. The soup tastes its best when blended and heated immediately before serving.

Hearty Bean Soup

This is the basic recipe for lentils, dried beans or split peas. Make it in large quantities, as it improves with age and can be used as a base for other soups.

1. Peel and chop onion and garlic. Wash and chop celery, leaves and all.
2. In a large soup pot, heat oil; then sauté onion, garlic and celery until golden.
3. Add stock or water, bay leaf and sage; bring to a boil. Wash and sort beans, then add to water and bring to boil again. Turn off heat and wait until beans sink to the bottom (about 15 minutes). If you have soaked beans overnight, this step may be omitted.
4. Simmer beans gently until tender. The time varies from 2 to 4 hours, depending on the type of bean. If you have a slow cooker (crock pot), a wood stove or an Aga with a very slow heat, let the soup cook overnight, or all day. It seems the longer this soup cooks, the better it tastes.
5. When beans are well cooked and beginning to get mushy, prepare the binding. Heat butter or oil in a small saucepan, add flour and cook slowly for 5 minutes, stirring occasionally. Then add water and salt and bring to a boil, stirring constantly. Pour into soup. If the soup has been cooked for a long, slow time, the binding may not be necessary. For a soup that has been cooked quickly, however, this is the step that really brings it together and gives the broth the long-cooked appearance. Another way to bind the soup is to spoon about a fourth of the beans into a blender, along with some broth, and purée it; then return to the soup.
6. Test soup for consistency. It should be thick, but not stiff. Add more water or stock if necessary.
7. Test for flavour. If water has been used instead of a rich stock, you may need to add some tamari, yeast extract or powdered vegetable broth.
8. Finally, test for saltiness. When you taste it, the soup should say "Yes! That's right." If it doesn't, try adding some salt.
9. Serve at a temperature which is piping hot yet doesn't burn the tongue.
10. Top with chopped parsley, grated cheese, or croûtons. Serve with a hot grain or fresh bread, to complement the protein.

Emergency

If the soup isn't done, and everyone has arrived for dinner, put the whole lot in a blender, purée it, then very carefully cook for a few more minutes, stirring constantly to avoid burning.
This soup isn't as lovely as the long-cooked one, but it will do at a pinch.

metric/imperial (6–8 servings)	american (6–8 servings)
1 onion	*1 onion*
4 cloves garlic	*4 cloves garlic*
4 stalks celery and leaves	*4 stalks celery and leaves*
2 Tbsp oil	*2 Tbsp oil*
2¼ litres/4 pints water	*2½ quarts water*
1 tsp sage	*1 tsp sage*
1 bay leaf	*1 bay leaf*
450g/1lb dried beans	*2½ cups dried beans*

binding

4 Tbsp butter or oil	*4 Tbsp butter or oil*
4 Tbsp flour	*4 Tbsp flour*
½ litre/1 pint water	*2 cups water*
3 tsp salt	*3 tsp salt*

Variations

This recipe is the base for an endless number of variations. After the beans are cooked add tinned tomatoes, chopped carrots, spinach, kale (thinly cut with scissors), cauliflower or broccoli, etc. Use what you have on hand.

To complement the protein, during the last of cooking add rice or barley.

Leftover vegetables can be added towards the end.

Cream of Cauliflower

metric/imperial (4 servings)
30g/1oz chopped onions
60g/2oz chopped celery and leaves
2 Tbsp butter or oil
450g/1lb cauliflower, washed and cut
*   into pieces*
water to cover
60g/2oz butter
4 Tbsp flour
½ litre/1 pint cooking water
salt
4 Tbsp milk or cream
4 egg yolks (optional)
parsley, nutmeg, paprika or hard
*   boiled egg for topping*

1. In a saucepan, heat the oil. Fry onions and celery until translucent.
2. Add water and cauliflower. Bring to a boil, then simmer until tender.
3. Draw water from cauliflower, saving the cooking liquid. Put a few florettes aside. Into a blender put cauliflower, onions, celery and enough water to purée easily. Blend until smooth.
4. In a saucepan, melt butter and whisk in the flour. Cook slowly for 5 minutes, stirring occasionally.
5. Add ½ litre/1 pint/2 cups cooking water. Simmer until thickened, stirring with a whisk.
6. Add puréed vegetables to sauce, taste soup, and add salt if needed.
7. Just before serving, add milk or cream and bring to serving temperature, being careful not to boil the soup.
8. (Optional) For added richness, stir a small amount of soup into beaten egg yolks; return to soup.
9. Put a few florettes in each soup bowl, then the soup. Top with nutmeg, paprika or chopped parsley.

american (4 servings)
¼ cup chopped onions
½ cup chopped celery and leaves
2 Tbsp butter of oil
1 medium cauliflower, washed and
*   cut into pieces*
water to cover
¼ cup butter
¼ cup flower
2 cups booking water
salt
¼ cup milk or cream
4 egg yolks (optional)
parsley, nutmeg, paprika or hard
*   cooked egg for topping*

Emergency

If you are really short of time, omit the step of making the sauce separately. After cooking the vegetables, put them with their cooking water plus butter and flour into the blender and purée everything. Return to saucepan and add water if needed; then cook for 5 minutes. Add milk and eggs, and serve.

Variations

This recipe can be used with many different vegetables; some good ones are asparagus, leeks, spinach, carrots, courgette (zucchini), mushrooms or cabbage. Use what you have. For a non-dairy soup, omit milk and eggs.

Caraway Seed Soup

A folk remedy – for winter, or for when you're out of sorts. It's presented in small quantity because this is the sort of soup you eat when you're alone, or that you make for someone who isn't feeling well.

1. In a small saucepan, heat oil and butter.
2. Add caraway seeds and stir them as they pop.
3. Mix in flour and cook over medium heat for about 3 minutes. Mixture should be dark, but not burned.
4. Slowly add hot water, while stirring. Bring to a boil.
5. Add salt. Taste, and add more salt of needed.
6. Top with croûtons and finely chopped parsley.

metric/imperial (2 servings)

1 tsp Caraway seeds
1 Tbsp oil
1 Tbsp butter
2 Tbsp flour
½ litre/1 pint hot water
¼ tsp salt
handful of croûtons
parsley

american (2 servings)

1 tsp Caraway seeds
1 Tbsp oil
1 Tbsp butter
2 Tbsp flour
2 cups hot water
¼ tsp salt
handful of croûtons
parsley

Garlic Soup

Good for what ails you.

1. Crush caraway seeds with a mortar and pestle.
2. Wash and chop potatoes. Simmer potatoes with caraway seeds in salted water.
3. When potatoes are mushy, add crushed garlic and butter.
4. Serve with croûtons on top.

metric/imperial

1 tsp caraway seeds
300g/10oz potatoes
1½ litres/2¼ pints water or stock
1 tsp salt
4 cloves garlic
1 Tbsp butter
croûtons

american

1 tsp caraway seeds
2 cups chopped potatoes
7 cups water or stock
1 tsp salt
4 cloves garlic
1 Tbsp butter
croûtons

A Different Minestrone

With salad and fresh bread, a satisfying peasant's meal.

1. Wash and chop vegetables.
2. In a soup pot, cover vegetables with water or stock and simmer until tender (about 30 minutes).
3. Meanwhile, slice onions in rings and quickly fry in olive oil until dark brown and crispy.
4. Grate cheese for topping.
5. When soup vegetables are tender, spoon about two-thirds into a blender: add some cooking water, process until smooth.
6. Pour purée back into soup pot. Mix soup, and check consistency. Add more water if needed.
7. Taste for salt; add some if necessary.
8. Pour into individual soup bowls. Top with sautéed onions and grated cheese.

Variation

For a non-dairy soup, substitute tamari roasted sunflower seeds for the cheese.

metric/imperial	american
Several vegetables in season	*Several vegetables in season*
(such as potatoes, carrots, courgettes,	*(such as potatoes, carrots, courgettes,*
green beans, onions, cabbage, squash, etc)	*green beans, onions, cabbage, squash, etc)*
water or stock	*water or stock*
½ onion per serving	*½ onion per serving*
olive oil	*olive oil*
parmesan cheese (whole if possible)	*parmesan cheese (whole if possible)*
salt	*salt*

Cream of Celery

This is a rich, non-dairy soup.

1. Wash and chop celery and leaves.
2. In a saucepan, sauté celery and leaves in oil.
3. When celery is beginning to become tender, add water, then simmer until tender.
4. Put sunflower seeds in blender with enough cooking water to cover and process until smooth.
5. Add celery, remaining cooking water and flour; blend for another minute, or until smooth.
6. For a very delicate soup, pass through a strainer.
7. Return to saucepan and simmer for five minutes, to allow flour to cook.
8. Add tamari and majoram. Taste for saltiness and add more tamari if needed.

Variation
Use any other vegetable in place of celery.

metric/imperial (4 servings)

60g/2oz sunflower seeds, cashews
or blanched almonds
225g/8oz celery and leaves
2 Tbsp oil, preferably corn oil
3 cups water
2 Tbsp flour
3 tsp tamari
1 tsp marjoram

american (4 servings)

½ cup sunflower seeds, cashews or blanched
almonds
2½ cups celery and leaves
2 Tbsp oil, preferably corn oil
3 cups water
2 Tbsp flour
3 tsp tamari
1 tsp marjoram

Egyptian Red Lentil Soup

We received a shipment of lentils labelled 'Egyptian red lentils' so we named this soup after them. It is a quick and easy one.

1. Bring water to boil.
2. Add lentils and simmer until mushy. (About 30 minutes)
3. Meanwhile, slice onion in crescents and quickly sauté in oil until brown.
4. Add tamari to soup. Let cook for another couple of minutes. As tamaris differ in strength, it is necessary to taste soup to see if amount is right.
5. Stir in sautéed onions and serve. (If serving in individual bowls, ladle the soup in, then top with onions.)

metric/imperial (6 servings)

2 litres/4 pints water or stock
455g/1lb red lentils
1 onion
2 Tbsp olive oil
4 Tbsp tamari (or less, if stock is used)

american (6 servings)

8 cups water or stock
2 cups red lentils
1 onion
2 Tbsp olive oil
¼ cup tamari (or less, if stock is used)

White Bean Soup with Artichokes

1. Wash and sort beans. Soak overnight in water.
2. Bring beans to a boil, then simmer for about an hour.
3. Meanwhile, prepare artichokes: cut into eighths and remove choke (whisker part in the middle) as well as the tougher outer leaves. Leave a good portion of the stem on. (Leftover outer leaves can be steamed separately for another meal.)
4. Add artichokes to the beans and continue simmering for another ½ hour, or just until beans are open and beginning to disintegrate, and artichokes are tender. Add more water, if needed, during cooking.
5. Make a paste of the peeled garlic, parsley, basil, olive oil and salt, by mashing well with a mortar and pestle. Add to soup at the very end of cooking, to preserve the fresh flavour of the seasonings.
6. Check consistency of soup. Add more water if needed. Add salt if needed.

metric/imperial

450g/1lb haricot beans, or any white bean
1.7 litre/3 pints water
2 globe artichokes
8 cloves garlic
60g/2oz parsley, chopped fine
2 tsp basil
6 Tbsp olive oil
3 tsp salt

american

2½ cups haricot beans, or any white bean
2 quarts water
2 globe artichokes
8 cloves garlic
1 cup finely chopped parsley
2 tsp basil
½ cup olive oil
3 tsp salt

Preparing Vegetables

The more food your body absorbs from the garden, the better.
As you eat, try always to think of all those who have helped
with the growing of the foodstuffs, the devas, the nature spirits,
the angels: by doing this you are showing your recognition and
appreciation for all that has been done
to help the things grow here.

—Eileen Caddy

In the very early days at Findhorn, Eileen Caddy received guidance that the produce from the garden they were creating would do them more good than anything bought, that it had tremendous life force in it, which was the main thing they needed.

In those beginning days, the enormous size of the plants in the vegetable garden drew visitors from far and wide, who were intrigued to hear of cooperation with nature and of the unity of all life. "But did anyone ever stop to think how difficult it is to cut up a forty pound cabbage?" laughed Eileen, recalling her rather unique challenges as cook for the community at that time.

Today, at the Findhorn Community, the cabbages have settled back down to normal, but the gardens still offer an abundance of vital, fresh vegetables. A lovely part of the daily routine for cooks is the cleaning and cutting of freshly gathered produce from our own land and from that of surrounding organic Scottish farms.

Choosing and preparing fresh produce can be a delightful part of daily living for people everywhere, although recognizing vibrancy and aliveness may be a tricky matter in these times, because of agricultural practices aimed at presenting the most cosmetically appealing product with the least amount of potential spoilage. Often, the largest and most colourful vegetables are only so because of being grown with chemicals, being dyed and waxed; their taste and vitality are disappointing. So have a discerning eye. Grow vegetables yourself if possible. If that is not possible, buy ones that have been grown by natural methods. And if you must use ordinary commercial vegetables, know that the care put into their preparation can improve their quality tremendously.

If possible, harvest vegetables immediately before preparing. If vegetables must be stored for a while, refrigerate them in an airtight container or bag, so their subtle flavour is protected from other surrounding flavours, and they are protected from the deteriorating effects of contact with air.

Wash vegetables quickly, and dry immediately afterwards. Many vitamins are water soluble; therefore it is a good idea that vegetables have as little contact with water as possible after they are harvested.

When you prepare vegetables, take enough time to allow a relationship to develop between you and them. Their strength and beauty as well as their life force can flow into you as you prepare them, if you are open to it. As you become more sensitive to their form and their grace, new ways of preparing the vegetables may suggest themselves to you.

The most important thing to remember is that the love and joy you put into the preparation can turn any potato into a prince.

Vegetable Cutting

*A simple dish takes on a special feeling when extra care
has been taken in cutting the vegetables*

Carrots can be cut diagonally, to reveal more of the inner pattern.
The diagonal cuts can then be piled up and cut again, to form
small matchsticks.

Celery butterflies are made by cutting the vegetable diagonally.

To wash leeks, chop off the end and any wilted leaves; then make
a small lengthwise slit in the leek, using the point of a small knife.
Wash out all dirt trapped inside. Cut leeks diagonally.

Garlic cloves can be peeled more quickly if each clove is first given
a blow with the side of a knife. This releases the skin.

To make uniform crescents from onions, cut the onion in half,
then begin slicing next to the cutting board and follow the growth
lines of the onion right around.

Cooking Methods

Steaming:

The most satisfactory method for cooking most vegetables is to steam them. This method preserves the natural flavour and nutrients. If you don't have a steamer pot, small stainless steel steamers which fit inside a regular saucepan are available at most wholefood shops. Put a small amount of water in a saucepan, wait for it to boil, then put in steamer with the vegetables in it. Cover and cook until vegetables are tender. For variety in flavour, after steaming toss vegetables in butter, tamari or fresh, chopped herbs.

Baking:

We're all accustomed to baking potatoes, but have you tried baking beetroot(beets), onions or winter squash?

Beetroot – Preheat oven to 220°C/Gas Mark 7/425°F. Wash beetroot and cut off their scrubby ends, but leave peels on. Place in baking dish and bake for 1–1½ hours (depending on their size). They are done when they can be easily pierced with a skewer. Serve with peels still on. They are crackly and sweettasting.

Onions – Preheat oven to 190°C/Gas Mark 5/375°F. Wash onions, but leave whole with the skins on. Bake in a baking dish for 1½ hours, or until they can be pierced with a skewer. To serve, remove skins by cutting off the end to which all the skin is attached and popping the onion out by pressing the skin. Serve with melted butter over them, or sautéed mushrooms. Garnish with chopped parsley.

Winter Squash – (This section is for Americans; I have not seen winter squash in Britain.) Butternut or acorn squash is ideal. Wash and dry the squash. Bake it whole at 375°F for at least 1 to 1½ hours, or until it can be pierced easily with a toothpick. When squash is done, remove it from the oven and split in half lengthwise. Scoop the strings and seeds from inside. Serve filled with melted butter and parsley, or with mushrooms sautéed in butter and garlic.

Baked Potatoes – For an easy, satisfying main dish, top baked potatoes with grated cheese, yogurt or soured cream, chopped chives and sautéed vegetables, such as mushrooms, green peppers, onions, courgettes, etc.

Sautéing:

This is especially good with cabbage, curly kale or other greens. Wash greens and chop, leaving water on leaves. Melt butter in a large saucepan, then add greens and stir while frying until butter is distributed evenly. Cover saucepan, lower heat and steam-fry until greens are tender, stirring occasionally so that they don't burn. Add caraway seeds or herbs at the end.

Stir-Frying:

To make the optimum use of fuel when it was scarce, the Chinese developed the method of stir-frying. Because the vegetables are cut very thin and are cooked by a combination of oil and steam, they are done very quickly. The valuable nutrients in the cooking water are consumed, because the water is thickened into a sauce. Although the classic seasoning for a stir-fried dish is garlic and ginger, other seasonings can be used as well. (A good dish is fried matchstick carrots, seasoned with cumin.) The proper pan to use for stir-frying is a wok with a lid. If you don't have one, use a large frying pan, or a saucepan, preferably with rounded corners. Vegetables that are particularly good in stir-fried dishes are long mung bean sprouts, snow peas, celery and mushrooms. When vegetables are cooked and sauce is finished, roasted cashews or roasted blanched almonds can be added. Cubed tofu is also very appropriate, and must be added at the end, so that the tofu is not broken up too much in the stir-frying. The method used in the following pages can be altered by using salt instead of tamari. In this case the sauce will be white instead of brown.

Stir Frying

1. Choose several vegetables which offer a variety of colour and texture. Vegetables often used in stir-fried dishes are snow peas, mung bean sprouts, mushrooms and celery.
2. Slice all vegetables very thin, then arrange on a plate or in separate bowls. Place together vegetables which take the same cooking time. Carrots and onions, for example, cook in about the same time, but mushrooms cook very quickly, so they will be kept apart and added at the end.
3. Finely chop garlic and grate ginger. Use 1 tsp of each for a small amount of vegetables.
4. Mix 2–8 Tbsp cornflour (cornstarch) or arrowroot with a small amount of cold water.
5. Have easily available garlic, ginger, vegetables, oil, tamari, water and cornflour mixture.
6. Put wok over high heat.
7. When it is hot add small amount of oil, and the garlic and ginger.
8. Add longer-cooking vegetables.
9. Quickly flip them around, to seal in the flavour.
10. Add a small amount of water.
11. Quickly cover the wok. Cook vegetables for a few minutes. Lower the heat if it sounds as though they are cooking so rapidly that they might burn.
12. Add remaining vegetables. The timing on this depends on what vegetables you have used and how thinly you have cut them. But estimate the difference in cooking time between longer-cooking and quickly-cooking vegetables, and add them so that all will be done simultaneously.
13. Mix vegetables in and replace cover.
14. Let vegetables continue to cook until they are crunchy done. The best way to test is to bite into a couple of them.
15. The next three steps must be done very quickly, so that vegetables neither burn nor overcook. Tilt wok so that cooking liquid all runs to one side. Add tamari to taste.
16. Give cornflour and water another little stir.
17. Then combine with cooking liquid.
18. Quickly stir sauce into vegetables, scooping under them to coat thoroughly. Sauce should be thickened just enough to cling to vegetables.
19. Taste sauce and add more tamari if needed, then more thickener if needed.

Serve immediately.

Main Course Savouries

*Your attitude when you eat anything should be one of joy and
pleasure and thanksgiving. You are to be constantly aware that
all these gifts are Mine.*

—*Eileen Caddy's guidance*

Vegetarian cookery does not strictly adhere to traditional classifications of main and side dishes. Often a very hearty soup or a salad serves as an entire meal. In other cases several vegetable dishes combine to make the main course. So, although the following are suggestions for 'main course savouries', remember that you can use 'main' and 'side' dishes almost interchangeably. In this way, cooking with vegetables is infinitely versatile, as we combine and recombine to create whole and satisfying meals.

The Simplest Supper

1. In a bowl, cover millet with boiling water. Wash around a bit, then drain. Repeat this procedure. (This hastens cooking of millet, and washes the grain as well.)
2. Bring milk to a boil. Add drained millet and salt; simmer for 20 minutes, or until tender.
3. Peel and chop onions. Sauté in oil until crispy and brown and very sweet-tasting.
4. Wash cabbage. Cut into quarters and remove hard core. Chop cabbage into bite-sized pieces, then steam.
5. To serve, put a spoonful of cabbage on each plate, and a spoonful of millet topped with sautéed onions.

metric/imperial (4 servings)

185/6½oz millet
570ml/1 pint milk
½ tsp salt
2 onions
2 Tbsp oil
1 head cabbage

american (4 servings)

1 cup millet
2½ cups milk
½ tsp salt
2 onions
2 Tbsp oil
1 head cabbage

Cauliflower Cheese

1. Preheat oven to 190°C/Gas Mark 5/ 375°F.
2. Wash cauliflower and break into flowerettes. Steam until not quite tender. Drain, reserving cooking water.
3. In a saucepan melt butter, then mix in flour, salt and mustard; slowly cook for at least 5 minutes, stirring constantly.
4. Gradually add liquid, stirring all the while; cook until mixture thickens. (Using cooking water instead of half of the milk gives the dish more of the cauliflower flavour.)
5. When sauce has thickened, add grated cheese and stir until melted.
6. Place cauliflower in greased baking dish and pour sauce over it.
7. Bake for 30 minutes or until sauce is bubbly and browned on top.

metric/imperial (4 servings)

510g/1½ lbs cauliflower, weighed without leaves
60g/2oz butter
4 Tbsp flour
½ tsp salt
½ tsp dry mustard
½ litre/1 pint milk, or half milk and half cauliflower cooking water
225g/8oz cheddar cheese, grated
paprika

american (4 servings)

1 large cauliflower
4 Tbsp butter
4 Tbsp flour
½ tsp salt
½ tsp dry mustard
2 cups milk, or half milk and half cauliflower cooking water
2 cups grated cheddar cheese
paprika

Mushroom Stuffed Peppers

1. Bring water to boil in a saucepan.
2. Cut peppers in half lengthwise. Remove stems and seeds. Drop into boiling water and cook, uncovered, for 4 minutes. Remove from water and allow to drain in a colander.
3. Brush or wipe mushrooms clean; then slice.
4. Chop parsley; slice Jerusalem artichokes.
5. Grate cheese.
6. Chop onions.
7. Melt part of the butter in a saucepan, then sauté onions until translucent.
8. Add remaining butter; then blend in flour, mustard and salt; cook over low heat for five minutes, stirring constantly.
9. Still stirring, blend in soured cream and cook until mixture thickens.
10. Remove from heat and add parsley, Jerusalem artichokes and sliced mushrooms.
11. Pile filling into pepper halves. Sprinkle grated cheese over top.
12. Place under grill (broiler) for about 5 minutes, or place on top rack in a very hot oven. Cook until cheese is bubbly. Serve immediately.

metric/imperial (6 servings)	american (6 servings)
3 large red bell peppers	3 large red bell peppers
225g/8oz fresh mushrooms	½lb fresh mushrooms
2 Tbsp chopped parsley	2 Tbsp chopped parsley
1oz Jerusalem artichokes	¼ cup Jerusalem artichokes
85g/3oz Gouda cheese	¾ cup grated jack cheese
3oz butter	6 Tbsp butter
1oz onion, finely chopped	¼ cup finely chopped onion
1½oz plain flour	6 Tbsp white flour
½ tsp dry mustard	½ tsp dry mustard
½ tsp salt	½ tsp salt
340ml/12floz soured cream	1½ cups sour cream

Heroic Cheese Soufflé

Dedicated to Sir George Trevelyan who gave the dish its name.

1. Melt butter in a saucepan. With a whisk, blend in flour until completely smooth. Add salt, mustard powder and cayenne; cook over low heat for at least 5 minutes, stirring all the while.
2. Turn heat up to moderate and, continuing to stir mixture with a whisk, slowly add milk. When sauce has thickened and is just beginning to bubble, remove from heat.
3. Add grated cheese and stir until cheese has melted. Let sauce cool.
4. Preheat oven to 180°C/Gas Mark 4/350°F.
5. Beat egg whites until stiff. Set aside.
6. Beat egg yolks slightly and add to cheese sauce, mixing thoroughly.
7. Barely fold egg whites into cheese mixture, using hands or a spatula. The lightness of the soufflé depends on the whites not being broken up very much.
8. Liberally rub the bottom and sides of a straight-sided baking dish with butter, then dust with flour. Try your various baking dishes until you find one that the soufflé fills at least ¾ full. As it bakes the soufflé will expand and create a golden puff rising out of the dish; hence its heroic quality.
9. Spoon mixture into baking dish; bake for 40 minutes or until soufflé is set and a knife inserted comes out clean.

metric (4–6 servings)	american (4–6 servings)
40g/1½oz butter	3 Tbsp butter
3 Tbsp flour	3 Tbsp flour
¼ tsp salt	¼ tsp salt
½ tsp mustard powder	½ tsp mustard powder
⅛ tsp cayenne	⅛ tsp cayenne
225ml/8floz milk	1 cup milk
225/8z cheddar cheese, grated	2 cups grated cheddar cheese
6 egg whites	6 egg whites
6 egg yolks	6 egg yolks

Tofu Teriyaki

1. Cut tofu into individual serving-sized slices, and drain; arrange in one layer in a glass baking dish.
2. In a blender place ginger, garlic, oil, mustard and apple concentrate. Blend until completely smooth; then add tamari and water and blend for a few more seconds.
3. Pour sauce over tofu; marinate for 2 hours.
4. Preheat oven to 210°C/Gas Mark 6/400°F.
5. Bake tofu in marinade for 20 minutes, or until piping hot.
6. Carefully remove tofu to a hot serving platter. Put platter in warm oven while sauce is being finished.
7. Pour sauce out of baking dish into a saucepan.
8. Dissolve arrowroot in cold water, then whisk into sauce as it heats. The correct amount of arrowroot varies, depending on how much liquid has been lost in the cooking, so add gradually until thickness suits your taste. Note: Arrowroot does not need to be cooked, as does cornflour or flour, so as soon as it thickens sauce may be served.
9. Pour sauce over tofu; garnish with parsley.

Note:

Various brands of apple juice concentrate and tamari differ in strength, so the flavour of this sauce may change each time you change brands. Therefore, to preserve the sweet-salt balance, add more concentrate or tamari as needed.

metric/imperial (6 servings)	american (6 servings)
1 kg/2lb tofu	2lb tofu
2 tsp grated fresh ginger	2½ tsp grated fresh ginger
5 cloves garlic	5 cloves garlic
2 Tbsp oil	2½ Tbsp oil
½ tsp dry mustard	½ tsp dry mustard
110ml/4floz apple juice concentrate	½ cup apple juice concentrate
110ml/4floz tamari	½ cup tamari
¼ litre/½ pint water	1 cup water
2 Tbsp arrowroot (approximately)	2 Tbsp arrowroot (approximately)
4 Tbsp cold water parsley	4 Tbsp cold water parsley

Moussaka

1. Peel and slice aubergines (eggplant). Sprinkle with salt. Allow bitter juices to drain for at least ½ hour. Pat aubergines dry.
2. Fry aubergine slices in olive oil. Drain.
3. Mix together walnuts, bread crumbs, wheat germ, pepper, egg and milk. Mixture should be moist.
4. Chop onions and mushrooms. Fry onions in oil and, when translucent, add mushrooms and continue frying until mushrooms are just tender.
5. To onions and mushrooms add nut mixture, tomato paste and cinnamon. Add water and cook over low heat for 10 minutes, stirring often. Add parsley.
6. Preheat oven to 190°C/Gas Mark 5/375°F.
7. Place alternate layers of aubergine and nut mixture in a greased baking dish, beginning and ending with aubergine.
8. Melt butter in a saucepan. Blend in flour, nutmeg and salt; then cook over a low heat for 5 minutes, stirring constantly. Blend in milk with a whisk, and cook over moderate heat, still stirring, until sauce thickens. Beat egg yolks in a bowl; mix a little of the sauce with yolks, then return mixture to sauce. Heat slightly but do not boil.
9. Pour sauce over aubergine layers.
10. Top with grated parmesan cheese.
11. Bake for 45 minutes, or until bubbly and browned on top.

metric/imperial (10 servings)	american (10 servings)
1.25kg/3lb aubergines	3lb eggplant
salt	salt
olive oil	olive oil
110g/4oz walnuts, ground	1 cup ground walnuts
30g/1oz bread crumbs	4 Tbsp bread crumbs
30g/1oz wheat germ	¼ cup wheat germ
¼ tsp pepper	¼ tsp pepper
1 egg	1 egg
4 Tbsp milk	4 Tbsp milk
2 onions	2 onions
170g/6oz mushrooms	2 cups sliced mushrooms
6 Tbsp tomato paste	6 Tbsp tomato paste
1 tsp cinnamon	1 tsp cinnamon
4 Tbsp water	4 Tbsp water
30g/1oz chopped parsley	½ cup chopped parsley
60g/2oz butter	4 Tbsp butter
4 Tbsp flour	4 Tbsp flour
½ tsp nutmeg	½ tsp nutmeg
¼ tsp salt	¼ tsp salt
½ litre/1 pint milk	2 cups milk
2 egg yolks	2 egg yolks
4 Tbsp parmesan cheese	4 Tbsp parmesan cheese

Mama Imperatore's Italian Tomato Sauce

Make this sauce in large quantity, then freeze part of it.

1. Separate garlic bulb into cloves; peel and finely mince.
2. Peel and chop onions.
3. In a large soup pot, sauté garlic, onions and herbs in oil.
4. Remove top from tomato tin, but leave contents in tin and cut tomatoes up by slicing through them several times with a knife.
5. Add tomatoes and tomato paste to onion mixture, as well as wine, salt and pepper, and soda.
6. Bring sauce to a boil, then reduce heat and simmer very slowly for at least 10 hours. Put asbestos pad or flame spreader between the pot and the heat; or, better yet, cook sauce in a crock pot (slow cooker) or on the slow section of an Aga or a wood stove. Check sauce occasionally to see that it isn't cooking too rapidly; add water if needed. Pot should be covered.
7. For the last two hours of cooking remove the lid, so that sauce can reduce and turn darker.
8. Serve sauce over pasta or polenta; or use in lasagne.

metric/imperial
Makes 25 servings: 3 litres/5 pints

1 bulb garlic
5–8 onions
olive oil
4 bay leaves
2 tsp basil
2 tsp oregano
2.6 kg/5lb 12oz tinned whole tomatoes
425 g/15oz tomato paste
¼ litre/½pint red wine
3 tsp salt
¼ tsp pepper
pinch of bicarbonate of soda (cuts acidity)

american
Makes 25 servings: 12½ cups

1 bulb garlic
5–8 onions
olive oil
4 bay leaves
2 tsp basil
2 tsp oregano
5lb 12oz canned whole tomatoes
15oz tomato paste
1 cup red wine
3 tsp salt
¼ tsp pepper
pinch of baking soda (cuts acidity)

Polenta

1. Stir together polenta, cold water and salt.
2. Bring water to boil in heavy saucepan or top of double saucepan. Add polenta mixture, stirring constantly.
3. Bring to boil, then simmer, stirring constantly, until thickened.
4. Preheat oven to 180°C/Gas Mark 4/ 350°F.
5. Rub a baking dish with butter.
6. Spoon in half the polenta, then sprinkle a layer of grated cheese, saving a little cheese for the top; then cover with remaining polenta and sprinkle with cheese.
7. Bake for ½ hour. Meanwhile heat the sauce.
8. Remove polenta from oven when done and let set for 5 minutes. Then slice in squares. Serve with sauce spooned over.

metric/imperial (4 servings)

170g/6oz polenta or maize meal
¼ litre/½ pint cold water
1 tsp salt
½ litre/1 pint boiling water
110g/4oz cheese, grated
½ litre/1 pint Italian tomato sauce (see previous page))

american (4 servings)

1 cup polenta or corn meal
1 cup cold water
1 tsp salt
2 cups boiling water
1 cup grated cheese
2 cups Italian tomato sauce (see pevious page)

Variation
Slice ½lb mushrooms
into tomato sauce while heating.

Vegetable Plait

metric/imperial (8 servings)	american (8 servings)

Filling: Part I

metric/imperial	american
110g/4oz celery	1 cup celery
340g/12oz potatoes	2 cups potatoes
270g/9½oz carrots	2 cups carrots
140g/5oz parsnips	1 cup parsnips
140g/5oz swede	1 cup swede (rutabaga)
140g/5oz green peas	2 cups green peas

Sauce

metric/imperial	american
1 onion	1 onion
4 cloves	4 cloves
1 bay leaf	1 bay leaf
570ml/1 pint milk	2½ cups pint milk
60g/2oz butter	¼ cup butter
60g/2oz flour	¼ cup flour
½ tsp salt	½ tsp salt
15g/½oz cheese, grated	2 Tbsp grated cheese

Filling: Part II

metric/imperial	american
2 onions	2 onions
oil	oil
110g/4oz cheese, grated	1 cup grated cheese

Pastry

metric/imperial	american
225g/8oz plain flour	2 cups plain flour
½ tsp salt	½ tsp salt
100g/3½oz margarine	7 Tbsp margarine
3 Tbsp ice cold water	3 Tbsp ice cold water
1 egg	1 egg
1 Tbsp water or milk	1 Tbsp water or milk

Gravy

metric/imperial	american
2 onions	2 onions
30g/1oz butter	2 Tbsp butter
2 Tbsp flour	2 Tbsp flour
570ml/1 pint stock	2½ cups stock
parsley for garnish	parsley for garnish

Filling: Part I

1. Wash and dice celery, potatoes, carrots, parsnips and swedes in 1cm(½ in) cubes. Leave peas whole.
2. Steam each vegetable separately until just tender. Do not allow to get mushy. If peas are frozen, just thaw, do not cook.
3. Drain vegetables well.

Sauce

1. With a knife make 6–8 slits in onion. Stud onion with cloves; insert a bay leaf in one of the slits.
2. Slowly heat milk for 15 minutes, with onion in it. Let milk cool slightly.
3. In a separate saucepan, whisk flour into melted butter, then cook for at least 5 minutes over medium heat, stirring constantly.
4. Slowly add milk through a strainer, while continuing to stir. Cook until sauce thickens; simmer, covered, for 15 minutes.
5. Stir in grated cheese until melted.

Filling: Part II

1. Dice onions and fry in oil until golden brown.
2. Grate cheese.

Pastry

1. Combine flour and salt; then work in margarine until texture of bread crumbs.
2. Add enough ice water that pastry can be gathered up in a ball.

Gravy

1. Slice onions in thin crescents.
2. Melt butter in a saucepan, then very slowly fry onions for ½ hour.
3. Stir flour in thoroughly, and continue cooking for at least 5 minutes.
4. Whisk in the stock. Increase heat and continue stirring until gravy thickens.
5. Add salt, if needed. If water has been used instead of stock, add a bit of tamari, Marmite, yeast extract or powdered vegetable broth to give flavour to the gravy.

Assembly

1. Preheat oven to 190°C/Gas Mark 5/375°F.
2. Mix vegetables with enough sauce to hold them together, without being sloppy.
3. On a floured surface, roll pastry into the largest rectangle possible.
4. At Findhorn we have very large baking pans and ovens, so we can put the whole pastry inside the pan. However, as you will probably be using a smaller pan and oven, fold the pastry in half, then carefully lift and unfold it over a flat baking tin, placing it so that the central part of the pastry is on the tin; the edges can extend beyond it, because they will eventually be folded over anyway.

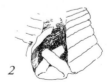

5. Cut pastry as shown in illustration N°1; strips should be about 2.5cm (1 inch) wide. There must be an equal number of wings on each side.
6. Spoon vegetable-sauce mixture into pastry, as neatly as possible. The sides of the

filling should slope in toward the top, and the filling should not extend to the part of the pastry which has been cut.

7. Sprinkle fried onions, then grated cheese over filling.
8. Plait (braid) pastry as shown in illustration N°2. Begin with the 'point' end of the arrow. Fold 'point' over filling, then alternate folding left and right wings over filling. Before reaching opposite end, fold end piece over filling.
9. Beat an egg with 1 Tbsp water or milk, and brush pastry with beaten egg.
10. Bake for ½ hour, or until nicely browned.

To Serve

Carefully remove plait to a serving platter. This will require two people and several spatulas. Garnish plait with parsley. Serve gravy in a separate dish. Slice plait for individual servings, and pour gravy over.

Variations

The vegetables we have used in the filling reflect middle-of-the-winter conditions in Scotland. Many other vegetables can be used in place of the predominantly root vegetables. Also, instead of using a variety of vegetables, a single one can be used, such as spinach or mushrooms.

Dutch Kale

Serve with sliced tomatoes topped with yogurt.

1. Butter Sauce: Melt butter slowly. Add tarragon and thyme. Simmer sauce very slowly until serving time. The long cooking time is necessary to achieve its nut-like flavour.
2. Wash potatoes; steam until tender.
3. Wash kale and remove leaves from stem, then steam until tender. Allow kale to cool, then chop very fine. If you wish, add some of the kale cooking water to the butter sauce.
4. Grate cheese.
5. Mash potatoes, allowing steam to evaporate, then thoroughly mix in kale, cheese, milk, pepper and egg yolks.
6. Beat egg whites until stiff, and fold into potato mixture.
7. Spoon into greased baking dish.
8. Bake at 190°C/Gas Mark 5/375°F for 30 minutes, or until hot and slightly browned on top.
9. To serve, spoon a portion onto a plate, make a little well in the potatoes and ladle sauce into the well.

metric/imperial (8 servings)	american (8 servings)
225g/8oz butter, unsalted if possible	1 cup butter, unsalted if possible
1 tsp tarragon	1 tsp tarragon
½ tsp thyme	½ tsp thyme
2kg/4lb potatoes	12 medium boiling potatoes
1kg/2lb kale	2lb kale
340g/12oz cheese, preferably Edam	3 cups grated cheese, preferably Edam
¼ litre/½ pint milk	1 cup milk
pinch of pepper	pinch of pepper
2 egg yolks	2 egg yolks
2 egg whites	2 egg whites

Lasagne

1. Drop lasagne noodles into boiling salted water one by one, and stir after each addition.
2. When noodles are not quite tender, remove from water one by one and lay on towel to drain.
3. Grate mozzarella cheese; combine with ricotta and beaten egg. Set aside.
4. Steam spinach until almost tender. Drain, then chop into large pieces.
5. Brush or wipe mushrooms clean. Slice.
6. Make bechamel sauce: in a saucepan, add flour to melted butter and cook for 5 minutes, stirring constantly. Increase heat and continue stirring while slowly adding milk. When sauce thickens, add nutmeg and salt. Remove from heat and stir in spinach and mushrooms.
7. Mix together parmesan cheese and bread crumbs.
8. To assemble lasagne: rub a large flat baking dish with butter, then lay one layer of noodles on bottom, followed by layer of one half of the tomato sauce, then noodles, ricotta mixture, noodles, bechamel sauce mixture, noodles, remaining tomato sauce, parmesan cheese and bread crumbs.
9. Bake at 180°C/Gas Mark 4/350°F for one hour, or until bubbly.

metric/imperial (6 servings)

340g/12oz lasagne noodles
½ litre/1 pint Italian tomato sauce
110g/4oz mozzarella cheese (or edam)
170g/6oz ricotta cheese (or cottage cheese)
1 egg
225g/8oz spinach
110g/4oz mushrooms
30g/1oz butter
2 Tbsp flour
¼ litre/½ pint milk
¼ tsp nutmeg
¼ tsp salt
30g/1oz parmesan cheese, grated
30g/1oz bread crumbs

american (6 servings)

12oz lasagne noodles
2½ cups Italian tomato sauce
1 cup grated mozzarella cheese
¾ cup ricotta cheese
1 egg
½lb spinach
2 cups sliced mushrooms
2 Tbsp butter
2 Tbsp flour
1 cup milk
¼ tsp nutmeg
¼ tsp salt
¼ cup grated parmesan cheese
¼ cup bread crumbs

Spinach Dumplings

Make these dumplings when you have some time the night before.

1. Wash spinach, and steam until tender. Drain.
2. Chop together (preferably in a blender or food grinder) the spinach, bread and cheese.
3. Beat eggs well and add to spinach mixture.
4. Add garlic powder, parmesan cheese, and salt and pepper to taste. Mix well.
5. Put mixture in a covered container, and refrigerate for at least 3 hours or overnight.
6. Roll spoonfuls of the mixture into small balls. Dip in flour; place on a plate.
7. Preheat oven to 190°C/Gas Mark 5/ 375°F.
8. Drop dumplings into boiling salted water. Cook until they float to the top (about 1 minute). Remove with tea strainer or slotted spoon. Drain.
9. Place dumplings in a greased casserole dish and cover with tomato sauce. Sprinkle with parmesan cheese; bake until bubbly.

metric/imperial (4 servings)

225g/8oz spinach
85g/3oz dry bread
85g/3oz cheddar cheese
2 eggs
¼ tsp garlic powder
30g/1oz parmesan cheese, grated
salt and pepper
flour
½ litre/1 pint Italian tomato sauce (see page 40)
15g/½oz parmesan cheese

american (4 servings)

8oz spinach (1 cup cooked)
2 slices dry bread
¾ cup grated chedaar cheese
2 eggs
¼ tsp garlic powder
¼ cup grated parmesan cheese
salt and pepper
flour
2½ cups Italian tomato sauce (see page 40)
2 Tbsp parmesan cheese

Leek & Mushroom Quiche

Pastry

1. Mix together the oats, flour, seeds, salt, mustard and grated cheese.
2. Cut in butter until well blended.
3. Add as much water as needed to hold pastry together.
4. With fingers press dough into a 23cm(9in) round pie tin. If you wish, refrigerate dough, in the tin, for an hour or more before baking.
5. Preheat oven to 220°C/Gas Mark 7/425°F.
6. Bake pastry for 15 minutes, or until browned. Remove from oven.

Filling

The filling can be started while pastry is being refrigerated, or as the pastry is baking.

1. Prepare leeks by making a lengthwise slit with a knife, and thoroughly washing out any dirt that might be trapped inside. Remove any wilted parts, then chop leeks into 2cm/¾in) segments.
2. Steam leeks until tender. Drain thoroughly.
3. Brush or wipe mushrooms clean, then slice.
4. Grate cheese and chop parsley very fine.
5. To shorten cooking time of quiche, scald the milk.
6. Beat eggs and salt, and combine with milk, mixing thoroughly.
7. Line bottom of pastry with leeks, followed by raw mushrooms, cheese and parsley. Pour egg-milk mixture over all. Sprinkle a bit of nutmeg on top.
8. Bake at 190°C/Gas Mark 5/375°F for 35 to 40 minutes, or until quiche is set and a knife inserted in the centre comes out clean.

Variations

For a more delicate quiche, use shortcrust pastry. (Recipe appears in Desserts section). Slice the vegetables very thin, then lightly sauté or steam. Allow vegetables to drain completely before adding to the quiche. For snacks or appetisers, make individual quiches in muffin tins.

metric/imperial (6 servings)

Pastry
40g/1½oz rolled oats
55g/2oz soft wholemeal flour
30g/1oz sesame seeds
½ tsp salt
¼ tsp dry mustard
30g/1oz cheese, grated
70g/2½oz butter
2 Tbsp water

Filling
200g/7oz leeks
110g/4oz mushrooms
55g/2oz cheese, grated
parsley
455ml/16floz milk
3 eggs
¼ tsp salt
nutmeg

american (6 servings)

Pastry
½ cup rolled oats
½ cup soft wholemeal flour
¼ cup sesame seeds
½ tsp salt
¼ tsp dry mustard
¼ cup grated cheese
⅓ cup butter
2 Tbsp water

Filling
2 cups chopped leeks
2 cups sliced mushrooms
½ cup grated cheese
parsley
2 cups milk
3 eggs
¼ tsp salt
nutmeg

Chickpea Casserole

This is a delicious way to use dry bread

1. Wash and sort chickpeas. Combine with water and sage in a saucepan. To reduce cooking time, soak beans overnight; otherwise, bring beans to a boil, then turn heat off and leave until chickpeas sink to the bottom. (About 15 minutes.) Bring to a boil again and simmer until completely tender. (About 2 hours.)
2. If possible, cut dry bread into cubes. Pour cooking water from beans over the bread and let bread completely soak up the water. Even the hardest pieces should soften. If there isn't enough water left from cooking the beans, add a little.
3. Preheat oven to 180°C/Gas Mark 4/ 350°F.
4. Sauté onions and celery in oil.
5. In a large mixing bowl mash chickpeas thoroughly, then add soaked bread and mash the two together. This can be done in an electric mixer or with a potato masher.
6. Add onions, celery, parsley, egg, cayenne, salt and tamari, and mix thoroughly. Taste for saltiness and add more tamari if needed.
7. Spoon into a greased baking dish and top with grated cheese.
8. Bake for 40 minutes or until golden brown.

metric/imperial (4–6 servings)

140g/5oz chickpeas
680ml/24floz water
½ tsp sage
170g/6oz dry bread
110g/4oz onion, chopped
110g/4oz celery and leaves, chopped
2 Tbsp oil
15g/½oz parsley, chopped
1 egg
¼ tsp cayenne
1 tsp salt
1 Tbsp tamari
110g/4oz cheese, grated

american (4–6 servings)

1 cup chickpeas (garbanzo beans)
3 cups water
½ tsp sage
2 cups dry bread
1 cup chopped onion
1 cup chopped celery and leaves
2 Tbsp oil
¼ cup chopped parsley
1 egg
¼ tsp cayenne
1 tsp salt
1 Tbsp tamari
1 cup grated cheese

Peter's Omelette

*For years we enjoyed Peter Caddy's delicious omelettes, and here we have his
step-by-step method. Make each person's omelette individually;
as each one can be made in less than thirty seconds, several can
be done very quickly. They are best when served immediately,
but if necessary can be kept warm for a few
minutes in a moderate oven.*

1. A secret to making good omelettes is to use a thick iron pan, to use it only for making omelettes and to keep it clean. If it is dirty, never wash it; rather heat it, fill it with salt, heat the salt for a minute or two, then empty the pan and wipe it out well with a dry cloth.
2. Beat eggs with salt and pepper in a bowl. Do not add water or milk.
3. Heat the pan over a very hot flame. When it is smoking, add a piece of butter about the size of a walnut.
4. Let butter melt, and just before the butter turns brown,
5. Pour in the eggs.
6. Shake pan forward and backwards with one hand, and with the other hand stir eggs with a fork.
7. Add a spoonful or two of filling. (See Fillings next page.)
8. Tip the pan and roll omelette down.
9. Let omelette sit for a moment, to firm.
10. Holding the plate at an angle, tip omelette out on to a plate.
11. Shape omelette with hands.

metric/imperial	american
3 eggs	*3 eggs*
⅛ tsp salt	*⅛ tsp salt*
pinch of pepper	*pinch of pepper*
butter	*butter*
filling	*filling*
Makes one omelette	*Makes one omelette*

Fillings

The following recipes each make enough for four omelettes.

Mushroom Filling

1. Wipe mushrooms clean, then slice.
2. Fry in butter until just tender. Add salt.

metric/imperial	american
455g/1lb fresh mushrooms	*8 cups fresh sliced mushrooms*
4oz butter	*8 Tbsp butter*
⅛ tsp salt	*⅛ tsp salt*

Tomato Cheese Filling

1. Peel and chop tomatoes.
2. Grate cheese.
3. Fill omelette with tomatoes, then sprinkle tomatoes with grated cheese.

metric/imperial	american
225g/8oz fresh tomatoes	*1 cup fresh chopped tomatoes*
110g/4oz cheese	*1 cup grated cheese*

Peter's Favourite: Aubergine Filling

1. Peel garlic. Peel and finely chop onion, aubergine and tomato. Wipe mushrooms clean, then chop. Wash and chop green pepper.
2. Melt butter in a frying pan. Put garlic through a garlic press; squeeze into frying pan. Add remaining vegetables and salt; slowly fry until completely tender, and almost sauce-like.

metric/imperial	american
1 clove garlic	*1 clove garlic*
60g/2oz onion	*½ cup onion*
110g/4oz aubergine	*1 cup eggplant (aubergine)*
60g/2oz fresh tomato	*½ cup fresh tomato*
60g/2oz fresh mushrooms	*1 cup fresh mushrooms*
60g/2oz green pepper	*½ cup green pepper*
60g/2oz butter	*4 Tbsp butter*
¼ tsp salt	*¼ tsp salt*

Loaf & Gravy

This is a dish that non-vegetarians find very satisfying.

Loaf

1. Cook lentils with sage in unsalted water. When done, drain and save excess water.
2. Cook rice and millet together in unsalted water.
3. Wash and chop onions, carrot and celery. Sauté in oil until tender.
4. Preheat oven to 180°C/Gas Mark 4/350°F.
5. In a large bowl, or with an electric mixer, combine all loaf ingredients. Mixture should hold together in a ball, but not be dry. Add lentils' cooking water if needed to moisten mixture. Emergency note: If you've let the mixture get too wet, that can be remedied by adding more maize meal (corn meal).
6. Taste for saltiness and add tamari if needed.
7. Place in oiled loaf pan. Bake for one hour.
8. Serve in slices, with gravy spooned over.

Gravy

1. Slice onions in thin crescents. (see Preparing Vegetables for instructions.) Sauté onions in oil.
2. Clean mushrooms with a brush or a cloth (do not wash them, as they absorb too much water). Slice mushrooms.
3. When onions are translucent, add mushrooms and continue cooking briefly until mushrooms are tender.
4. Add water, basil and bay leaf. Bring to a boil, then reduce heat to simmer.
5. Mix cornflour (cornstarch) and cold water together until completely smooth. Slowly add to simmering gravy, stirring constantly, until gravy thickens to your liking.
6. Add tamari to taste. This is a thick, hearty gravy, reminiscent of non-vegetarian gravies. As tamaris differ in strength, it is necessary to add a little bit at a time, tasting all the while.
7. Let sauce simmer very gently, covered, for 20 minutes.

metric/imperial (10 servings)	american (10 servings)
140g/5oz green lentils	*¾ cup lentils*
½ tsp sage	*½ tsp sage*
140g/5oz brown rice	*¾ cup brown rice*
140g/5oz millet	*¾ cup millet*
1 onion	*1 onion*
1 carrot	*1 carrot*
2 stalks celery and leaves	*2 stalks celery and leaves*
2 Tbsp oil	*2 Tbsp oil*
30g/1oz maize meal	*¼ cup corn meal*
30g/1oz almonds or cashews, chopped	*¼ cup chopped almonds or cashews*
½ tsp thyme	*½ tsp thyme*
½ tsp salt	*½ tsp salt*
1 Tbsp tamari	*1 Tbsp tamari*
15g/½oz fresh parsley, chopped fine	*2 Tbsp chopped fresh parsley*

Gravy

Gravy

1 onion	*1 onion*
2 Tbsp oil	*2 Tbsp oil*
225g/8oz mushrooms (very ripe mushrooms give more flavour)	*2 cups sliced mushrooms (very ripe mushrooms give more flavour)*
570ml/1 pint water	*2½ cups water*
½ tsp basil	*½ tsp basil*
1 bay leaf	*1 bay leaf*
6 Tbsp cornflour or arrowroot	*½ cup cornstarch or arrowroot*
110ml/4floz cold water	*½ cup cold water*
3-5 Tbsp tamari	*3–5 Tbsp tamari*

Peasant Pie

Instructions for Pastry

1. Mix together flour, salt and sesame seeds.
2. Cut in shortening until dough resembles small peas.
3. Add enough buttermilk to bring pastry together in a ball. This part can be done in advance, and, in fact, the pastry is easier to work and is flakier if it has been chilled for a while. Remove from refrigerator 30 minutes before using, if it has been chilled for a long time.

Instructions for Filling

1. Mix soured cream and dill together. Set aside.
2. Hard-cook the eggs. Peel and slice.
3. Clean the cabbage, cut in quarters, remove the hard core, then chop cabbage into bite-sized pieces. Steam until barely tender. Drain well.
4. Prepare leeks by making a lengthwise slit with a knife, and thoroughly washing out any dirt that might be trapped inside. Remove wilted parts. Chop leeks into bite-sized segments, and sauté in butter and lemon juice until tender. Drain.
5. Slice mushrooms and leave them raw.
6. Mix together cabbage, leeks, mushrooms, basil, tarragon and marjoram. Taste the mixture and add salt if needed.

Assembly

1. Preheat oven to 205°C/Gas Mark 6/400°F.
2. Roll out ⅔ of the pastry dough and fit into bottom and sides of a medium-sized baking dish.
3. Spread soured cream-dill mixture over bottom of pie, followed by sliced eggs, then vegetable mixture.
4. Roll out remaining ⅓ of pastry dough and place on top of pie, joining it to bottom crust by pinching edges together.
5. Make decorative slashes in top of pie, so that steam can escape.
6. Bake for 15 minutes, then lower heat to 180°C/Gas Mark 4/350°F, and continue baking for 20 minutes more, or until light brown.

metric/imperial 6 servings

Pastry
115g/4oz flour
½ tsp salt
2½ Tbsp sesame seeds
55g/2oz shortening
140ml/3 Tbsp buttermilk or
    soured milk

Filling
5floz soured cream
¼ tsp dill
4 eggs
455g/1lb cabbage
170g/6oz leeks or onions
30g/1oz butter
1 Tbsp lemon juice
225g/8oz mushrooms
¼ tsp basil
¼ tsp tarragon
¼ tsp marjoram

american 6 servings

Pastry
1 cup flour
½ tsp salt
3 Tbsp sesame seeds
⅓ cup shortening
3 Tbsp buttermilk or soured
    milk

Filling
¾ cup sour cream
¼ tsp dill
4 eggs
1 small head cabbage
2 leeks or onions
2 Tbsp butter
1 Tbsp lemon juice
½lb mushrooms
¼ tsp basil
¼ tsp tarragon
¼ tsp marjoram

see variations for this recipe on following page...

Variations

The basic ingredients of a peasant pie are vegetables, a sauce and a pastry crust. The variations are endless. Once you have become familiar with preparing the pie, try using different vegetables. Or for another change of flavour, in place of the soured cream substitute a white sauce or any other sauce or gravy.
(This is a good way to use left-overs.)

Spinach Beans

1. Wash and sort beans. Combine with sage and water and bring to a boil, then remove from heat until all beans have sunk to the bottom. Once again bring to a boil, then simmer until tender (about 1½ hours). Drain beans, saving the cooking water.

2. Chop onions and celery; finely chop garlic.

3. In a large saucepan heat olive oil, then sauté garlic for a minute. Add onions and celery; continue to sauté until tender.

4. Add cooking water, salt, pepper, parsley, basil to onion mixture; cook for 10 minutes.

5. Stir in the beans, then lay spinach over the top.

6. Put top on the saucepan and steam until spinach is done. It may be necessary to add water.

7. Stir spinach into bean mixture, then spoon into serving dish.

8. Sprinkle parmesan cheese over all, and serve.

metric/imperial (6 servings)

170g/6oz white kidney beans or any white bean
½ tsp sage
680ml/24floz water
2 onions
3 stalks celery
4 cloves garlic
3 Tbsp olive oil
½ tsp salt
pinch of pepper
2 Tbsp chopped parsley
½ tsp basil
455g/1lb spinach
30g/1oz parmesan cheese, grated

american (6 servings)

1 cup white kidney beans or any white bean
½ tsp sage
3 cups water
2 onions
3 stalks celery
4 cloves garlic
¼ cup olive oil
½ tsp salt
pinch of pepper
2 Tbsp chopped parsley
½ tsp basil
1lb spinach
¼ cup grated parmesan cheese

Indonesian Meal
by Erik

Nasi goreng (fried rice), marinated tofu with
peanut sauce, garlic bananas, sambal oelek (hot sauce),
salad and garnishes.
Fresh papaya, with a slice of lemon, is
suggested for dessert.

All the elements of this meal will make 8 servings, except for the sauce,
where the recipe is for a large amount.

Sambal Oelek

If you live near Indonesian food stores, you can purchase this sauce. This
recipe is for a large amount; stored in a clean container in the freezer the
sauce will keep almost indefinitely.

1. Peel tomatoes and chop fine.
2. Grate rind from one lemon; juice both lemons.
3. Wearing rubber gloves, chop peppers very fine. Wash gloves and hands immediately afterwards, and be careful not to touch face with hands, as peppers are very strong.
4. Put peppers in saucepan with water. Bring to a boil, then add tomatoes and simmer for 10 minutes.
5. Chop shallots very fine. Break garlic bulbs into cloves; peel cloves, then squeeze through a press and chop what remains in the press.
6. Fry shallots in small amount of oil. When transparent add garlic and fry until golden.
7. Add shallots and garlic to peppers, as well as sugar, salt, soya sauce, lemon juice and rind.
8. Bring to a boil and stir while boiling for 15 minutes.
9. Reduce heat, cover and simmer for 4–5 hours. Be careful not to burn sauce. Put an asbestos pad or a heat spreader between saucepan and heat. If sauce gets too thick, add water. If not thick enough, boil for a few minutes. When finished, sauce should be consistency of jam or marmalade. Store in a clean container with a tight lid.

metric/imperial	american
12 tomatoes or 18 tinned tomatoes, drained	12 tomatoes or 18 canned tomatoes, drained
2 small lemons	2 small lemons
20 rawit peppers (very hot, small red peppers)	20 rawit peppers (very hot, small red peppers)
1 litre/1½ pints water	4 cups water
15 shallots	15 shallots
4 bulbs garlic	4 bulbs garlic
2 tsp sugar	2 tsp sugar
2 tsp salt	2 tsp salt
¼ litre/½ pint sweet Chinese soya sauce	1 cup sweet Chinese soya sauce

Salad

This can be made a day in advance.

1. Wash and chop all vegetables into very small cubes.
2. Combine with yogurt, lemon juice, and salt and pepper to taste.
3. Place in a covered container in a cool place for at least four hours.

metric/imperial	american
1 carrot	1 carrot
110g/4oz cauliflower	¼ of a medium-sized cauliflower
½ cucumber	½ cucumber
1 red bell pepper	1 red bell pepper
2 Tbsp chopped fresh parsley	2 Tbsp chopped fresh parsley
chives	chives
2 gherkin pickles	2 gherkin pickles
¼litre/½ pint yogurt	1 cup yogurt
juice of ½ lemon	juice of ½ lemon

Tofu

1. Cut tofu into chunks and arrange in one layer in a glass baking dish.
2. Put remaining ingredients in a blender and process until smooth. Pour over tofu and marinate for 2–3 hours.
3. Bake tofu at 210°C/Gas Mark 6/400°F for 30 minutes, or until piping hot.
4. Serve tofu with peanut sauce (see next page) spooned over.
5. Strain leftover marinade, and use for another meal.

metric/imperial	american
680g/24oz tofu	4½ cups tofu
¼ litre/½ pint tamari	1 cup tamari
¼ litre/½ pint water	1 cup water
3 cloves garlic	3 cloves garlic
15g/½ oz ginger root	3 tsp grated ginger root

Peanut Sauce

1. Grate rind of lemon, then juice it. Grate orange rind.
2. Finely chop onion and garlic; grate ginger root.
3. Sauté onion in oil. When tender, add garlic and ginger; fry lightly.
4. Thin peanut butter with hot boiling water until it is the thickness of running honey.
5. Gently heat peanut butter in a heavy saucepan or in the top of a double saucepan over boiling water
6. Add onions, garlic, ginger, lemon juice and rind, orange rind, sambal oelek, soya sauce and sugar.
7. Mix thoroughly; then taste to see if salt is needed before adding it.
8. Simmer for ½ hour. Do not allow to boil. Add more water if sauce gets too thick.

Emergency

If by some mistake sauce separates because it has been allowed to boil, mix a little arrowroot with cold water and add to sauce.

metric/imperial	american
1 tsp lemon rind	1 tsp lemon rind
1 Tbsp lemon juice	1 Tbsp lemon juice
1 tsp orange rind	1 tsp orange rind
1 onion	1 onion
5 cloves garlic	5 cloves garlic
1 tsp grated ginger root	1 tsp grated ginger root
oil	oil
225g/8oz smooth peanut butter	1 cup smooth peanut butter
boiling water	boiling water
1 tsp sambal oelek (hot sauce)	1 tsp sambal oelek (hot sauce)
2 Tbsp sweet Chinese soya sauce	2 Tbsp sweet Chinese soya sauce
2 tsp brown sugar	2 tsp brown sugar
½ tsp salt	½ tsp salt

Garnishes

1. Preheat oven to 180°C/Gas Mark 4/350°F.
2. In separate pans, roast peanuts and coconut, turning often. When roasted, mix together.
3. Serve on the table in bowls, or sprinkle over food on served plate.

metric/imperial	american
280g/10oz peanuts	2 cups peanuts
90g/3oz coconut	1 cup coconut

Garlic Bananas

1. Peel and slice bananas.
2. Place bananas, lemon juice and garlic powder in electric mixer bowl and whip at a slow speed for ½ hour. This process is what gives the dish its characteristic fluffiness.
3. Put banana mixture into greased flat baking dish.
4. Bake at 170°C/Gas Mark 3/335°F for 20 minutes.

metric/imperial	american
8 very ripe bananas	8 very ripe bananas
juice of ½ lemon	juice of ½ lemon
3 Tbsp garlic powder	3 Tbsp garlic powder

Nasi Goreng

1. Bring water to a boil. Wash rice and drain.
2. Add rice and salt to boiling water. Bring to a boil again, then reduce heat and simmer, covered, for 40 minutes, or until rice is just tender. Do not overcook.
3. Wash and chop vegetables. Leave peas whole. Peel tomatoes before chopping. Garlic should be minced and vegetables should be thinly sliced to cook quickly. Experiment with different kinds of cutting, to accentuate the beauty of the vegetables.
4. In a wok or frying pan, fry onions in oil. When tender, add garlic and ginger, then remaining vegetables and seasonings. Add a few drops of water; cover wok.
5. When vegetables are tender, stir in hot rice.
6. Rice can be kept warm in a covered dish in a moderate oven, or served immediately.

metric/imperial	american
¾litre/1½ pints water	3 cups pints water
340g/12oz brown rice	1½ cups brown rice
¼ tsp salt	¼ tsp salt
1 large onion	1 large onion
3 cloves garlic	3 cloves garlic
3 tsp grated ginger root	3 tsp grated ginger root
1 large carrot	1 large carrot
3 red bell peppers	3 red bell peppers
45g/1½ oz parsley, chopped fine	¾ cup finely chopped parsley
170g/6oz peas	1 cup peas
170g/6oz bamboo shoots	¾ cup bamboo shoots
1 firm tomato	1 firm tomato
oil	oil
3 tsp sambal oelek (or more)	3 tsp sambal oelek (or more)
2 tsp sugar	2 tsp sugar
pinch of turmeric	pinch of turmeric

Salads

*When you make a salad, as you handle each vegetable or herb,
let your mind dwell on how each was made. You can feel the
struggle that some of them have had to pull through, whereas
with others you can feel the ease and freedom in which they have
been brought to fruition. All these thoughts and feelings are
important. They bring the very life force into your body.*

—Eileen Caddy's guidance

For nearly eight years, Peter, Eileen and Dorothy – the founders of the community – lived almost exclusively on the produce grown in their own small garden. Eileen's daily spiritual guidance instructed them to take in the high vibrations of their vegetables to transform their physical bodies into light bodies. Not understanding what that meant at the time, but willing to comply, Peter squeezed as many plants into their tiny plot as possible. Every day they ate huge salads with sometimes as many as twenty different fresh vegetables and herbs in them.

Fresh salads are still a part of meals at the Findhorn Foundation; the salad table makes a glowing mandala of each day's harvest. Often the last minutes of preparation before a meal are spent putting the final decorative touches on deep bowls of grated beets, carrots and sprouts.

If you have a garden, a lovely daily ritual is the gathering of fresh vegetables and herbs for salads. Whereas salads are delicious when simple – lettuce with olive oil, lemon oil and a few herbs – they can also expand to include nearly every vegetable and often to take a more important role as the central part of a meal.

Salads are enhanced by tasty dressings, made colourful by the edition of edible flowers and various garnishes. Sprouted beans and grains add variety and nourishment, and have the advantage of being available year-round.

Eating fresh raw vegetables strengthens and purifies us for the tasks ahead; it can give us a delightful daily contact with the nature kingdoms and with the life force that comes through them.

Preparing Salad

Many vegetables which wouldn't ordinarily be considered for salads make perfect salad additions when grated. Root vegetables, such as beetroot (beets), turnips and Jerusalem artichokes, are particularly good. They should be grated just before serving.

Make a salad vegetable of tough winter greens by cutting them very thin with scissors.

Edible wild plants and flowers can be added to the salad for variety.

To make salad preparation easier, wash salad greens when you have a few minutes, then wrap them, with the moisture still on the leaves, in a towel. Keep in the refrigerator until needed.

Dressings

Mayonnaise

1. Put all ingredients into a blender jar, using 2 Tbsp oil to begin.
2. Process at low speed; with blender running, remove the small inner part of the lid and very slowly drizzle in oil. Keep adding oil, and as mayonnaise begins to thicken, remove lid and watch it. As it whirls around there will be a hole in the centre. The second that the hole closes, stop adding oil immediately. If the mayonnaise is to be used as salad dressing, it is finished at this point.

   Emergency: If the whole thing falls apart, as it sometimes does, pour the dressing out of the blender, break another egg into the blender, then slowly add the fallen-apart dressing to the egg, with the blender running. Only add it until the hole closes, then STOP. (You probably added too much oil the first time, and that's why it fell apart.)
3. If you would like an even thicker mayonnaise, remove from blender and whisk in more oil by hand, adding it very slowly.

metric/imperial	american
4 eggs, room temperature	*4 eggs, room temperature*
1 tsp dry mustard	*1 tsp dry mustard*
1 tsp salt	*1 tsp salt*
¼ tsp cayenne	*¼ tsp cayenne*
2 Tbsp vinegar	*2 Tbsp vinegar*
oil	*oil*

Variation

We used to have a lot of friendly competition to see who could come up with the most outrageously flavoured mayonnaise. Bobananda won the competition and goes down in history for his carob mayonnaise (add carob powder to taste to above recipe). For more conventional flavours, blend the basic recipe with spring onions, garlic, parsley, cucumber, tomatoes or your favourite herb.

Tomato Yogurt Dressing

1. Purée all ingredients in a blender. The dressing should be thick and creamy.
2. If you wish a thinner dressing, add milk.

metric/imperial (¾ litre/1¼ pints)

3 tomatoes
½ litre/1 pint yogurt
3 large sprigs of parsley
1½ tsp basil
1½ tsp oregano
1½ tsp garlic powder
1½ tsp celery powder
1 tsp salt (optional)

american (¾ quart)

3 tomatoes
2 cups yogurt
3 large sprigs of parsley
1½ tsp basil
1½ tsp oregano
1½ tsp garlic powder
1½ tsp celery powder
1 tsp salt (optional)

Honey Tamari Dressing

1. Chop onions.
2. With a whisk, blend oil, lemon juice, tamari, honey and cayenne.
3. Add onions and sesame seeds. Whisk a bit more.
4. Before serving, whisk the dressing again.

metric/imperial

2 Tbsp finely chopped spring onion
455ml/16floz safflower oil
110ml/4floz lemon juice
225ml/8floz tamari
3 Tbsp honey
¼ tsp cayenne
2½ Tbsp sesame seed

american

2 Tbsp finely chopped green onion
2 cups safflower oil
½ cup lemon juice
1 cup tamari
4 Tbsp honey
¼ tsp cayenne
3 Tbsp sesame seeds

Chartres Cathedral Dressing

When Paul makes this salad dressing, it takes him three hours, observers say, and he uses the same care and concentration that went into the building of Chartres Cathedral. One thing he regularly does is make a mistake and add too much of something, so much of the three hours is spent in correcting the mistake but the salad dressing comes out even better in these cases for some reason. So make some mistakes and take three hours and you've got the dressing. Or you can just whip it together in a few minutes. It's still good.

1. Pour lemon juice and orange juice through a strainer into a jar.
2. Add remaining ingredients and shake the jar.

Serving Suggestion:
This goes well over a salad of lettuce and avocado; or a spinach salad with tomato, cucumber and bits of hard-boiled egg, chopped fine.

metric/imperial (1 litre/2 pints)	american (1 quart)
¼ litre/½ pint lemon juice	1 cup lemon juice
¼ litre/½ pint orange juice	1 cup orange juice
½ litre/1 pint oil	2½ cups oil
3 tsp mustard powder	3 tsp mustard powder
1½ tsp garlic powder	1½ tsp garlic powder
½ tsp parsley	½ tsp parsley
¼ tsp paprika	¼ tsp paprika
2 tsp marjoram	2 tsp marjoram
¼ tsp salt	¼ tsp salt
4 tsp sugar	4 tsp sugar
pinch of pepper	pinch of pepper
pinch of cayenne	pinch of cayenne

Tahini Dressing

The simplest dressing, yet one of the best.

1. Add water to tahini and whisk until water is completely absorbed and tahini has become fluffy.
2. Add tamari to taste.
3. For a thinner dressing, add more water.

metric/imperial (½ litre/1 pint)	american (2 cups)
¼ litre/½ pint tahini	*1 cup tahini*
¼ litre/½ pint cold water	*1 cup cold water*
about 2–3 Tbsp tamari	*about 2–3 Tbsp tamari*

Essence of Sprouts Dressing

1. Peel garlic.
2. Process all ingredients in blender until smooth.
3. Refrigerate dressing and use within two days.

Variation
For a different taste, instead of adding sprouts, add parsley, chives, cucumber or tomato.

metric/imperial	american
4 cloves garlic	*4 cloves garlic*
340 ml/12floz olive oil	*1½ cups olive oil*
110ml/4floz lemon juice	*½ cup lemon juice*
3 Tbsp tamari	*3 Tbsp tamari*
110g/4oz alfalfa or bean sprouts	*2 cups alfalfa or bean sprouts*

Garnishes

These little additions can give a plain salad real pizazz.
They're also great with soup.

Garlic Croûtons

1. Cut bread into cubes, then spread out on an ungreased baking tin.
2. Bake at the lowest heat in your oven for 1–2 hours, or until bread is dry and hard. Or if you are in a hurry, bake at 180°C/Gas Mark 4/350°F for about ½ hour, stirring frequently.
3. For plain croûtons, the process is finished at this point. Store croûtons in an airtight container.
4. Just before serving time, peel and chop garlic, then sauté in butter.

<u>Variation</u>
For herb croûtons, sauté dry croûtons in butter with 1 tsp herbs added:
such as basil, oregano, marjoram or thyme. Or sauté them in
4 Tbsp olive oil, ⅛ tsp salt and 1 tsp herbs.

metric/imperial	american
170g/6oz bread	*4 slices bread*
4 cloves garlic	*4 cloves garlic*
60g/2oz butter	*4 Tbsp butter*

Gomasio

The favourite condiment for everything.

1. Heat a heavy frying pan over a high flame.
2. When frying pan is hot, add seeds, lower heat and roast seeds, stirring occasionally, for just a few minutes, or until they are beginning to turn golden. Add salt and continue roasting until seeds are done (when they crush easily and taste completely roasted).
3. When seeds and salt have cooled, grind in a mortar and pestle or a nut grinder. They should be ground to a powder, with a few seeds left whole for flavour.
4. Store in an air-tight jar. Make in small amounts, so that it can be used within a week.

metric/imperial	american
Seven parts sesame seeds one part salt	*Seven parts sesame seeds one part salt*

Tamari Nuts

Spread peanuts in one layer in a large baking tin. Place on the bottom rack of the oven and roast at 180°C/Gas Mark 4/350°F for 30–60 minutes, stirring occasionally. When nicely browned, remove from oven and immediately sprinkle tamari over nuts, while stirring with a wooden spoon. Add enough tamari that they taste salty, but not so much that there is tamari left in the pan. The tamari should all evaporate as they are stirred.

Variations

Use the same method for cashews, almonds, sunflower seeds, pumpkin seeds. Sprinkle with ground ginger, garlic powder or onion powder.

Seaweed

Yes, you read it right: sea-weed.
It's delicious when prepared well, full of nutrients, and people tend to crave it after discovering they like it. And it's a great side garnish with a salad, or with rice. If you live near a source of fresh sea-weed, by all means use it. Otherwise, you can obtain it in its dried form from wholefood shops. Even the severest critics usually like sea-weed prepared this way.

1. In a saucepan, cover sea-weed with water. Simmer, covered, until tender. The time varies greatly, depending on the type of sea-weed. It is done when tender, like lasagne noodles. Test it with your fingernail. If the smell of the sea-weed cooking is more than you can bear, start frying the onion, garlic and ginger, to cover the smell. (Confessions of a former sea-weed detester.)
2. Drain sea-weed and chop into bite-sized segments.
3. Peel and finely chop onion and garlic. Fry onion, garlic and ginger in oil until tender.
4. Add sea-weed and fry a half minute longer, then mix in tamari.

metric/imperial	american
30g/1oz sea-weed	1½ cups sea-weed
1 onion	1 onion
4 cloves garlic	4 cloves garlic
2 tsp grated ginger	2 tsp grated ginger
oil	oil
1 Tbsp tamari	1 Tbsp tamari

Sprouts

Watching something grow out of that tiny seed, seeing a small green bit pop out, is a never-ending miracle. Mung beans, alfalfa seeds, chick peas, aduki beans, fenugreek seeds, radish seeds, wheat: almost any whole natural seed, bean or grain will sprout.

To grow sprouts, soak seeds overnight, then leave them in indirect light, rinsing twice daily until ready. Please remember that essential simplicity to the process. Here we describe everything in detail, this is because the sprouts inspired us, not because the process is complicated. And the rewards of growing sprouts are many. Not only do salads become more filling, satisfying and nourishing, but handling sprouts is a daily reminder that the life force is at work.

1. Put seeds in a jar. (Seeds can be obtained at wholefood shops. They must be live, and not chemically treated.) For alfalfa seeds, use 3 Tbsp for a 1 litre/2 pint/1 quart jar. (For all other seeds and beans, fill the jar ¼ full.) We use the jars that are available to us, but it would be better to use a wide mouth jar, for ease in draining water later.
2. Fill jar half full with cold water.
3. Leave seeds to soak overnight.
4. In the morning, put a piece of cheesecloth or lacy material on the jar. The mesh must be large enough to let the water out easily, but not so large that the seeds escape.
5. Fasten the cheesecloth on very securely with a rubber band, as the seeds will be rinsed many times, and it is very disheartening to have a whole jar of seeds empty into the sink because the top has come loose.
6. Pour off soaking water and drain.
7. Leave seeds in indirect light, preferably at 30° tilt, so that any excess water can run out. Put them where they are easily accessible and visible, so that you will remember to rinse them. Some people leave them in the dish drainer. Sprouts must have even temperature and light to grow well. In the summer protect them from too much heat and sun; in the winter give them more light and warmth. NOTE: If you want to grow Chinese style long mung bean sprouts, grow them in complete darkness.
8. To rinse sprouts, fill jar with water.
9. Gently shake seeds and water around.
10. Drain water.
11. Leave bottles upside down for a few minutes, to let all the water drain; then return them to their growing spot. Continue rinsing sprouts twice a day until they are ready to be eaten.

...continued over

12. Sprouts are ready to be eaten when they have lost all their starchiness, and taste like a vegetable. This will take from one to ten days, depending on the type of sprout and the climate where you live. Try eating the sprouts at different lengths, to see what seems the most agreeable to you. Sunflower seed sprouts, however, should always be used before the sprouted part is as long as the seed. Alfalfa sprouts should be quite a bit longer than the others, and are ready when you can see two little leaves growing at the end of the sprout.
13. Note: The remainder of the process applies only to alfalfa sprouts. When sprouts have grown two leaves, put into a pan of cold water.
14. Gently break up any solid masses that may have developed.
15. Swish sprouts around in the water.
16. Scoop off hulls that float to the top.
17. When all hulls have been scooped off, pour water through a colander.
18. Some hulls also will have sunk to the bottom. Carefully pick sprouts from the hulls.
19. Now put the hulled sprouts into a larger jar, so that they have more room to grow. Or divide them between two jars.
20. Put on a mesh cover.
21. Leave them upside down in a window where they will receive a lot of light, but not direct sunlight (although we do put them in direct sunlight here in Scotland, because the climate is cool). When they have turned green, they are ready to eat.

Breads

Before, in the old, food provided the energy for building or maintaining a solid physical body, but now, in the new, it is the life force, the light which one absorbs that matters.

—Eileen Caddy's guidance

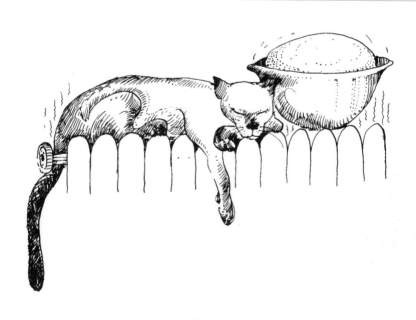

There's no denying the pleasure of baking bread: the smell in the house, the feeling of the dough under your hands, the delight in eating it and sharing it with family. It's another way to put love into the food you prepare.

We use wholemeal flour in most of our bread. If you've never used it before, try growing accustomed to it slowly by first mixing it half and half with white. Wholemeal flour, like other whole grains, takes longer to bake than its refined counterpart. For bread baking, a strong, or hard, flour should be used. For pastries and cakes, use a soft flour.

If baking for a small family seems too much bother, note that most of these recipes are for large quantities: you put almost an equal amount of energy into the process, and half the bread can be frozen for later use.

How do you know when the bread is done? For the beginner it can be a mystery. It should, of course, be golden brown on the outside. When removed from the baking tin, it should give a hollow sound when tapped on the bottom with a fist. Some can tell by the smell when the bread is done. If you're really in doubt, cut your first experimental loaves in half and inspect the inside. After two or three such inspections, you should begin to get a sense of what the bread looks like when it's done.

Basic Wholemeal Bread

1. Dissolve yeast in enough warm water to cover. Add honey; do not stir. Let sit until yeast 'mushrooms' (5 minutes or so).
2. Sift dry ingredients together.
3. When yeast looks frothy, stir well and add to flour mixture.
4. Add water until flour comes together into dough. Work with hands until the sides and bottom of the bowl are clean.
5. Work in oil; then knead for 5–10 minutes, until dough is supple, uniform in appearance, and 'fleshy' like an ear lobe or a baby's bottom.
6. Oil a bowl and place dough in it. Cover with a damp cloth and place in a warm spot in your kitchen or even a steamy bathroom. Let rise until double in size (about 1½ h hours).
7. Oil bread pans now, or flat sheets for braids or rolls.
8. After bread doubles, punch it down well with your fist and let it sit for 10 to 15 minutes more.
9. Form dough into loaves and allow to rise for 30 minutes.
10. Bake at 210°C/Gas Mark 6/400°F for 45–55 minutes, or until done.

metric/imperial (4 mediam loaves)	american (4 medium loaves)
20g/¾oz dried yeast	*3 Tbsp dried yeast*
warm water	*warm water*
2 Tbsp honey	*2 Tbsp honey*
3.2kg/7lb wholemeal bread flour (or half wholemeal and half unbleached white)	*25 cups whole wheat bread flour (or half whole wheat and half unbleached white)*
2–3 Tbsp salt about	*2–3 Tbsp salt*
2 litres/3 pints warm water	*about 2 quarts warm water*
3 Tbsp oil	*3 Tbsp oil*

Shaping the Loaves

*The time of shaping and decorating the bread can be your favourite time,
and a moment for creativity and inspiration to flow.
Here are some ideas to begin with.*

Regular Loaf
Press dough into rectangle, fold in thirds. Press again
in a rectangle, fold in thirds in the opposite direction.
Press out again, then roll up and place in loaf pan,
seam side down.

Round
Knead dough into round shape. Make slashes in
top with sharp knife.

Diagonal Cuts
Make regular loaf, then make diagonal slashes in
top of loaf with sharp knife or dough knife.

Rolls
To make rolls a uniform size, weigh each piece of
dough before forming the roll.

Clover Leaf – 3 little balls of dough in oiled muffin tins.

Circular Twist – Make two strips of dough, and join at
either end. Then twist in opposite directions, and curl
around so that ends meet. Pinch together.

Round – Make balls of dough, then cut decorative slashes
on top. Or sprinkle with poppy or sesame seeds.

Bake at 220°C/Gas Mark 7/425°F for about 20 minutes, or
until browned.

3 Plait (Braid)
Done just like plaiting hair.

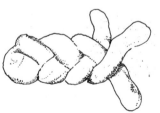

Decorative additions
To any of these loaves or rolls, add a shiny crust
by brushing with beaten egg to which 1 Tbsp
water has been added. Sprinkle poppy seeds or
sesame seeds over the top.

Variations for Wholemeal Bread

Cheese Bread
Roll out dough to a rectangular shape, and liberally spread grated cheese on it, leaving top and bottom edges with an empty margin. Start at top and roll dough into loaf. Place in pan as for a regular shaped loaf.

Cheese Plait
Work grated cheese into the dough (about 110g/4oz/1 cup for one loaf of bread), then cut into pieces for plaiting, as described previously. Cheese plaits are beautiful and very popular. Brush with egg wash and sprinkle with poppy or sesame seeds.

Herb Bread
Have about 3 or 4 favourite savoury herbs (1 tsp each) soaking in water. Some that do well are basil, thyme, rosemary, marjoram, sage or dill (the last two should be used sparingly as they are so strong). Roll out dough into a rectangle and spread with butter or margarine, then sprinkle drained soaked herbs on bread. Roll up bread and place in oiled pan. Brush with egg wash and sprinkle with seeds.

Cinnamon Raisin Bread
Have 85g/3oz/½ cup raisins soaking in hot water. Roll dough out in a rectangular shape, and spread with butter. Sprinkle drained raisins and 1 tsp cinnamon over all. Start at top and roll it tightly. Dab bottom edge with water to make dough stick together, and prick across the seam. Gently place, seam side down, in oiled loaf pan and brush with a glaze of 1 Tbsp melted butter, 1 Tbsp honey and ¼ tsp cinnamon. This loaf takes a little longer to bake than regular wheat bread. Check it after 50–60 minutes.

Sourdough Bread

Starter
1. Mix flour and enough warm water to make a soupy mix. Let stand in covered container in refrigerator for as long as you like, from overnight to months. The longer it sits, the riper and more sour (and perhaps more tasty) the bread.

Bread
1. Dissolve yeast in enough warm water to cover it. Add honey. Let sit for a few minutes, or until the yeast mushrooms on its own, without stirring.
2. Mix flour and salt together.
3. Stir yeast mixture thoroughly and add to flour and salt.
4. Add this fairly dry mix to the starter (which is fairly wet) then slowly add flour or water until dough is of a consistency to be kneaded easily. Knead dough for about 10 minutes, or until consistent and spongey.
5. Place in oiled bowl and cover with damp cloth. In a warm place, let rise until double in size (about 1½ hours).
6. Punch it down thoroughly, and let rise again, about ½ hour.
7. On a floured board, form into French style loaves by rolling a piece of dough with open hands until long and evenly shaped.
8. Place on oiled baking sheet, brush with egg wash (egg and a little water mixed well) and make diagonal slits in top of bread with sharp knife.
9. Bake at 170°C/Gas Mark 3/325°F for 45–50 minutes, or until light golden brown and hollow sounding on bottom when tapped.

metric/imperial (1–2 loaves)	american (1–2 loaves)
Starter	Starter
450g/1lb wholemeal bread flour	*3½ cups whole wheat bread flour*
warm water	*warm water*
Bread	Bread
1 Tbsp dry yeast	*1¼ Tbsp dry yeast*
60g/2oz honey	*3 Tbsp honey*
450g/1lb wholemeal bread flour	*3½ cups whole wheat bread flour*
¾ Tbsp salt	*1 Tbsp salt*
about 1 litre/2 pints water	*about 1 quart water*

Unleavened Flowers-Seed Bread

Unleavened breads fit nicely into a busy schedule, as they are left for 8–12 hours, or overnight, and finished later.

1. Mix together dry ingredients and seeds
2. Add water slowly, adding just enough to make dough come together to be kneaded. Watch the consistency as you mix it. It won't be fluffy and spongey like yeasted bread, but heavier and somewhat soft. Mix well.
3. Knead for 5 to 10 minutes, on a floured surface.
4. Place dough in oiled bowl, cover with damp towel; leave in a warm place for 8–12 hours, or overnight.
5. In the morning, knead for 5 minutes or so, working in the crusty top part of the dough.
6. Shape into loaves, then dip into poppy seeds. Place in an oiled loaf pan.
7. Bake at 170°C/Gas Mark 3/325°F for 1½ hours, or until crust on top is golden brown.
8. Cut bread very thin to serve.

metric/imperial (1–2 loaves)	american (1–2 loaves)
1kg/2lb 6oz wholemeal bread flour	*8½ cups whole wheat bread flour*
1 Tbsp salt	*1 Tbsp salt*
2 Tbsp sesame seeds	*2½ Tbsp sesame seeds*
6 Tbsp poppy seeds	*⅓ cup poppy seeds*
5 Tbsp sunflower seeds	*⅓ cup sunflower seeds*
about ¾ litre/1½ pints water	*about 3 cups water*
poppy seeds	*poppy seeds*

Soda Bread

A bread which can be made in surprisingly little time; the taste of soda bread brings memories of the warm people and inviting hearths of Ireland.

1. Preheat oven to 230°C/Gas Mark 8/450°F.
2. Grease a flat baking tin.
3. Combine dry ingredients. Make a little well and add honey, if using; then slowly add milk while mixing into flour with a fork. Add just enough milk that mixture comes together into a dough.
4. Knead briefly, then shape into round loaf. Place on baking tin and cut a cross all the way across the top and down the side with a sharp knife.
5. Brush top of loaves with beaten egg to which 1 Tbsp water has been added.
6. Bake for 15 minutes, then reduce heat to 180°C/Gas Mark 4/350°F and bake for another 15 minutes, or until done.

Variations

Add 1 tsp cinnamon or cardamom to dry ingredients.
Sprinkle top of loaf with sesame or poppy seeds.

metric/imperial (1 loaf)	american (1 loaf)
455g/1lb bread flour	3½ cups bread flour
¾ tsp bicarbonate of soda	1 tsp baking soda
¾ tsp salt	1 tsp salt
¾ tsp sugar or honey	1 tsp sugar or honey
¼ litre/½ pint sour milk or buttermilk	1 cup sour milk or buttermilk
1 egg	1 egg

Honey Buns

1. Dissolve yeast in a small amount of warm (not hot) water. Add honey, and let mixture sit without stirring for 5 minutes, or until bubbly.
2. In a large bowl thoroughly beat together eggs, oil, honey, water, milk powder and salt.
3. Add the yeast and about half of the flour. With a wooden spoon and then by hand, work in the remaining flour. Mix and knead adding as much flour as needed to keep dough from sticking. Knead for about 15 minutes, or until small bubbles begin to appear on surface of dough.
4. Cover with damp cloth and let rise in a warm place until double, about 1½ hours. Punch down and let rise again, about an hour.
5. For filling, slowly melt butter; when warm, remove from heat and whisk in honey and cinnamon. Mix well.
6. Divide dough in half. Roll each half out in a large rectangle, about 1cm(¼in) thick and 46cm(18in) long. Spread filling over all, then sprinkle raisins. Starting with long side, roll rectangle tightly, and seal edge by pinching. Cut each roll into 18 slices and place nine rolls each in four 20cm(8in) round baking tins. Let rise until double.
7. Bake at 190°C/Gas Mark 5/375°F for 20–25 minutes, or until browned.
8. Melt butter for topping. Remove from heat and whisk in remaining topping ingredients; mix well. When rolls have cooled, drizzle topping over them.
9. Optional: Sprinkle buns with chopped walnuts, slivered almonds or coconut.

metric/imperial (36 rolls)	american (36 rolls)
Sweet Roll Dough	**Sweet Roll Dough**
2 Tbsp yeast	*2 Tbsp yeast*
1 tsp honey	*1 tsp honey*
2 eggs	*2 eggs*
110ml/4floz oil	*½ cup oil*
170g/6oz mild white honey	*½ cup mild white honey*
455ml/16floz warm water	*2 cups warm water*
60g/2oz milk powder	*½ cup milk powder*
2 tsp salt	*2 tsp salt*
1kg/2lb 4oz wholemeal bread flour, or half wholemeal and half unbleached white	*8 cups wholemeal bread flour, or half wholemeal and half unbleached white*
Filling	**Filling**
110g/4oz butter	*½ cup butter*
170g/6oz honey	*½ cup honey*
1 Tbsp cinnamon	*1 Tbsp cinnamon*
85g/3oz raisins	*½ cup raisins*

continued over.......

Topping (Optional)
60g/2oz butter
85g/3oz honey
30g/1oz milk powder
¼ tsp vanilla

Topping (Optional)
¼ cup butter
¼ cup honey
¼ cup milk powder
¼ tsp vanilla

Variations

The basic sweet roll dough can also be used for dinner rolls. See *Shaping The Loaves* section for roll shapes and baking instructions. For another breakfast roll, try Bill's Cardamom Buns. Follow steps 1–4 of the basic recipe, except add 2 Tbsp ground cardamom to the dough (it's especially tasty if the cardamom is freshly ground). After dough has risen twice, break off small pieces of dough and make a rope 25cm(10in) long and 1.5cm(½in) in diameter. Bring two ends together and pinch, making a shape like an oxen's yoke. Dip one surface of the roll first in melted butter, then in sugar. Place, sugar side up, on a greased baking tin. Let rise until puffy.

Bake at 210°C/Gas Mark 6/400°F for 20 minutes or until browned.

Bran Muffins

Serve with butter and cream cheese.

1. Pour boiling water over raisins to soak them. Set aside.
2. Preheat oven to 210°C/Gas Mark 6/400°F.
3. Grease muffin tins.
4. Mix dry ingredients together. Set aside.
5. Beat eggs, then add oil, honey, molasses and milk and mix thoroughly. (Honey and molasses will not stick to the measuring jug if oil has been measured in it first.)
6. Combine dry ingredients with molasses mixture. Just mix together; do not over-beat.
7. Drain raisins; fold them into batter.
8. Fill muffin tins two-thirds full with batter. Bake for 20–25 minutes, or until muffins spring back when pressed with a finger.

metric/imperial (36 large muffins)	american (36 large muffins)
225g/8oz raisins	*1½ cups raisins*
510g/18oz soft wholemeal flour	*4 cups whole wheat pastry flour*
140g/5oz bran	*4 cups bran*
2½ tsp baking powder	*3 tsp baking powder*
2½ tsp bicarbonate of soda	*3 tsp baking soda*
1¼ tsp salt	*1½ tsp salt*
3 eggs	*3 eggs*
170ml/6floz oil	*¾ cup oil*
170ml/6floz honey	*¾ cup honey*
170ml/6floz molasses	*¾ cup molasses*
455ml/16floz milk	*2 cups milk*

Shelley's Bagels

1. Heat potato water to 32°C(90°F). Add yeast and honey to water and let stand for 5 minutes; then mix until dissolved.
2. Combine milk powder, salt and flours.
3. Add oil to yeast mixture, then gradually add flour mixture until dough is stiff. Add more flour if needed.
4. Turn dough onto floured board and knead for 10 minutes.
5. Let rise until double (about 1½ hours).
6. Punch down and knead again for a few minutes.
7. Roll out pieces of dough to 15cm x 2cm (6in x ¾in). Bring ends around to form a circle. Pinch ends together, then smooth the seam.
8. Add 1 Tbsp sugar to 2 litres/3 pints/2 quarts boiling water.
9. Add bagels, a few at a time, to boiling water. They will sink to the bottom. When they rise to the top, turn over and continue to boil for 30 seconds.
10. Drain water, then place on greased baking sheet and brush with beaten egg.
11. Bake at 230°C/Gas Mark 8/450°F for 20 minutes, or until browned on both sides.

Variations

Maize meal (corn meal) can be used to replace ⅛ of the amount of either flour.
Before baking, top bagels with finely chopped onion, garlic, sesame seeds, poppy seeds or coarse salt.

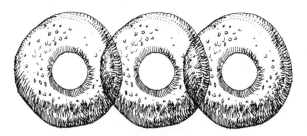

metric/imperial (30 bagels)	american (30 bagels)
680ml/24floz potato cooking water (or plain water)	3 cups potato cooking water (or plain water)
2 Tbsp dry yeast	2 Tbsp dry yeast
110–170g/4–6oz honey	⅓–½ cup honey
225g/8oz milk powder	2 cups milk powder
2 tsp salt	2 tsp salt
510g/18oz wholemeal flour	4 cups whole wheat flour
510g/18oz unbleached white flour	4 cups unbleached white flour
110ml/4floz oil	½ cup oil
1 egg	1 egg

Breakfasts

Why, sometimes I've believed as many as six impossible things before breakfast.

—Lewis Carroll
Alice Through the Looking Glass

Eggs à la Moray Firth

1. Preheat oven to 180°C/Gas Mark 4/350°F.
2. Grease baking dish.
3. Wash tomatoes; cut out stems and middle part.
4. Salt and pepper tomatoes.
5. Grate cheese and sprinkle half of it into the tomatoes.
6. Put tomatoes into baking dish. Into each one put a bit of butter, then break an egg into it. Salt the egg, sprinkle with remaining cheese, and top with a sprinkling of chopped parsley.
7. Bake for 20–25 minutes, or until eggs are cooked.

metric/imperial (4 servings)	american (4 servings)
4 large tomatoes	4 large tomatoes
salt and pepper	salt and pepper
30g/1oz Swiss cheese	¼ cup grated Swiss cheese
30g/1oz butter	2 Tbsp butter
4 eggs	4 eggs
parsley	parsley

Hot Cereal

Did you know that nearly any grain can be ground and used as a breakfast cereal? Some popular ones are rice, millet, corn, and a rice-millet mixture.

1. Heat water and salt in the top of a double saucepan.
2. Meanwhile, grind rice in a grain grinder or a blender. It should be just a bit coarser than flour.
3. With a whisk, stir grain into water. Place over boiling water and cook for 20 minutes, or until tender. By cooking cereal in a double saucepan, cleaning the pan is a lot easier. Also, you don't have to watch over the cereal and stir it all the time; so you're free to make the rest of the breakfast or to take a shower.
4. Check the consistency of the cereal; add more water if needed. Cook another minute and serve.

Variations

For a very filling cereal, substitute milk for the water. To make these cereals for infants, use twice as much liquid. Whole grain cereal is very satisfying on its own, but if you'd like to add toppings, here are some ideas: Sweet nuts, dried fruit, fresh fruit, seeds, cinnamon, butter, honey. Savoury tamari, butter, steamed greens, sprouts.

metric/imperial (4 servings)	american (4 servings)
680ml/24floz water	3 cups water
1 tsp salt	1 tsp salt
200g/7oz rice	1 cup rice

Muesli

Prepare muesli in bulk; then it's always ready for a quick breakfast.

1. Chop dried fruit. (To avoid a sticky knife when chopping fruit, first dip knife in solid butter.)
2. Mix all ingredients together and store in an airtight container.
3. Muesli is usually not cooked, but is eaten as is, topped with, for example, fresh fruit and milk, or apple purée and kefir.
4. To aid the digestibility of muesli, soak overnight in milk, water or apple juice.
5. If you are unable to obtain wheat, rye or barley flakes, substitute oats.

metric/imperial	american
340g/11oz dried fruit (such as apricots, raisins, dates, figs, sultanas or a mixture)	*2 cups dried fruit (such as apricots, raisins, dates, figs, sultanas or a mixture)*
340g/11oz nuts (such as walnuts, cashews, almonds, hazelnuts; use nuts that are fresh)	*2 cups nuts (such as walnuts, cashews, almonds, hazelnuts; use nuts that are fresh)*
455g/1lb porridge oats,	*6 cups rolled oats*
85g/3oz wheat flakes	*1 cup wheat flakes*
85g/3oz rye flakes	*1 cup rye flakes*
85g/3oz barley flakes	*1 cup barley flakes*
30g/1oz bran	*¾ cup bran*
30g/1oz coconut	*¼ cup coconut*
60g/2oz sunflower seeds	*½ cup sunflower seeds*

Granola

Granola is much like muesli, except that it is sweetened and roasted in the oven.

1. Preheat oven to 210°C/Gas Mark 6/400°F.
2. With a whisk, mix together honey, oil, salt and vanilla.
3. Combine remaining ingredients except for dried fruit. Add oil-honey mixture to dry ingredients, but do not mix very much.
4. Pour into greased flat baking tins and bake for 30 to 60 minutes, stirring occasionally. While granola is baking, chop dried fruit; add it about 10 minutes before the end of baking. Granola is ready when golden brown and toasty. If you prefer granola that is sweeter, add more honey.
5. Cool completely, then store in an airtight container.
6. Serve with fresh fruit and yogurt.

metric/imperial	american
140ml/5floz oil	1¼ cups oil
340g/12oz honey	1 cup honey
1½ tsp salt	1½ tsp salt
1 tsp vanilla essence	1 tsp vanilla
680g/1½lb rolled oats	9 cups rolled oats
85g/3oz wheat flakes	1 cup wheat flakes
85g/3oz rye flakes	1 cup rye flakes
85g/3oz barley flakes	1 cup barley flakes
200g/7oz nuts	1½ cups nuts
85g/3oz sesame seeds	½ cup sesame seeds
60g/2oz sunflower seeds	½ cup sunflower seeds
30g/1oz coconut	¼ cup coconut
400g/14oz dried fruit	2½ cups dried fruit

Scrambled Tofu

1. Drain tofu well.
2. Peel and finely chop onion. Wash and finely chop green pepper.
3. Sauté onion and green pepper in oil.
4. When vegetables are completely tender, mix in tofu. As it is already cooked, it only needs to be heated through.
5. Add tamari to taste and serve immediately.

metric/imperial	american
455g/1lb tofu	*2 cups tofu*
1 onion	*1 onion*
1 green pepper	*1 green pepper*
2½ Tbsp oil	*3 Tbsp oil*
about 2 Tbsp tamari	*about 2 Tbsp tamari*

Apple Purée

1. Wash, core and chop apples.
2. In a saucepan combine apples, cloves, cinnamon and lemon rind. Add enough water that apples can cook without sticking. Simmer apples until mushy, stirring occasionally.
3. If you wish, purée apples through a strainer.
4. Add butter and honey. Mix well.
5. Serve immediately, or store in a covered container in the refrigerator for later use.

metric/imperial	american
5 cooking apples	*5 cooking apples*
4 whole cloves	*4 whole cloves*
1 cinnamon stick	*1 cinnamon stick*
1 tsp grated lemon rind	*1 tsp grated lemon rind*
1 Tbsp butter	*1 Tbsp butter*
2 Tbsp honey or brown sugar (optional)	*2 Tbsp honey or brown sugar (optional)*

Variation: APPLE SNOW
A quick and simple dessert, makes 8 servings

Instructions
1. Make apple purée using 4 Tbsp honey; let it cool.
2. Beat 2 egg whites until stiff; then fold into purée. Pour into serving dish.
3. Refrigerate for at least 2 hours before serving.

Kefir

Kefir is cultured, somewhat like yogurt; yet it has the advantage that it does not require heating, so it is a raw milk product.
Kefir is usually drunk rather than eaten. In order to make it, it is necessary to have kefir grains, which are obtainable at some wholefood shops.

1. Combine grains and milk in a perfectly clean jar.
2. Find a safe place to leave the jar at room temperature (21°C/70°F) for two to three days. Kefir is ready when the milk has thickened.
3. Pour kefir through a sieve. As Kefir grains are damaged by contact with metal, use a plastic or wooden sieve. Stir kefir in the sieve (with a wooden spoon) until all the kefir has drained through and only grains are left. The kefir can be eaten immediately, or refrigerated for later use.
4. Wash grains under cold running water. Let them drain, then put in a clean jar and fill with milk for a new batch of kefir.

Some notes about kefir

1. If you must use pasteurised milk, strain the kefir grains and wash them daily.
2. For a thinner kefir, use fewer grains.
3. Kefir is milder when left for a shorter time. For a strong, almost alcoholic kefir, leave for seven days.
4. Kefir grains will multiply. Give some away to your friends.
5. Make a refreshing blender drink with kefir and fruit.

metric/imperial	american
1 litre/2 pints milk, preferably raw	*1 quart milk, preferably raw*
½ tea cup kefir grains	*½ cup kefir grains*

Fresh Fruit with Tahini Sauce

1. Mix all sauce ingredients together thoroughly.
2. Wash and chop fruits. Serve topped with sauce and sunflower seeds.

Variation: Use fresh fruit in season

metric/imperial	american
Sauce	Sauce
1 Tbsp tahini	*1 Tbsp tahini*
1 tsp molasses	*1 tsp molasses*
juice of 1 orange	*juice of 1 orange*
Fruit	Fruit
1 apple	*1 apple*
1 banana	*1 banana*
1 Tbsp dried fruit	*1 Tbsp dried fruit*
1 Tbsp sunflower seeds	*1 Tbsp sunflower seeds*

Homemade Yogurt

1. Be sure that all equipment used is very clean.
2. Heat milk to 75°C/170°F.
3. Blend powdered milk into milk. Adding powdered milk makes the yogurt thicker, and is a shortcut for the traditional method of heating milk for ½ hour.
4. Allow mixture to cool to 45°C/115°F, then add prepared yogurt and stir well. Do not succumb to the notion that if you use more starter, the yogurt will be thicker. In fact, there is a supersaturation point and the yogurt can be thinner.
5. Place yogurt in clean jars in a place where a temperature of 43°–48°C (110°–120°F) can be maintained. Too high a temperature will kill the bacteria and too low a temperature will not support growth. The shorter the incubation time (usually dependent on temperature), the sweeter the yogurt.
6. Yogurt is ready when it has become thick. That should take about four hours.
7. Yogurt is best when eaten within a day or two of being made. Folk wisdom says that the culture improves if it is used more often; so it's a good idea to make small batches and make it often. Refrigerate yogurt in covered container.

metric/imperial
1 litre/2 pints milk
60g/2oz milk powder
1½ Tbsp plain yogurt (commercially pre-
    pared, or saved from your last batch)

american
1 quart milk
½ cup milk powder
1½ Tbsp plain yogurt (commercially pre-
    pared, or saved from your last batch)

Yogurt Sundae

1. Spoon yogurt into a large dish. Slice banana over it, then drizzle honey and sprinkle on granola.
2. Slice fresh fruit and arrange over yogurt. Top with chopped walnuts, raisins, sunflower seeds and coconut. If you have a fresh strawberry, put it on the top.

metric/imperial
(1–2 servings)

225ml/8floz yogurt
1 banana
1 Tbsp honey
4 Tbsp granola
140g/5oz fresh fruit in
    season
30g/1oz walnuts
30g/1oz raisins
1 Tbsp sunflower seeds
1 Tbsp grated coconut

american
(1–2 servings)

1 cup yogurt
1 banana
1 Tbsp honey
4 Tbsp granola
1 cup fresh fruit in
    season
¼ cup walnuts
¼ cup raisins
1 Tbsp sunflower seeds
1 Tbsp grated coconut

Baked Apples

1. Preheat oven to 210°C/Gas Mark 6/400°F.
2. Wash and core apples; then make a slit around the middle (so that top can rise while baking).
3. Chop walnuts, mix with currants, honey, flour, ginger, cinnamon, salt and vanilla.
4. Melt butter and stir enough into mixture to moisten. Mix thoroughly.
5. Stuff mixture into apples.
6. Place apples in a greased baking dish and bake for 30-40 minutes, or until completely tender. Serve hot or cold. If you wish, top with yogurt.

metric/imperial (6 servings)	american (6 servings)
6 cooking apples	6 cooking apples
30g/1oz walnuts	¼ cup walnuts
30g/1oz currants	¼ cup currants
3 Tbsp honey or demerara sugar	¼ cup honey or brown sugar
30g/1oz soft flour	¼ cup pastry flour
⅛ tsp ginger	⅛ tsp ginger
½ tsp cinnamon	½ tsp cinnamon
pinch of salt	pinch of salt
drop of vanilla	drop of vanilla
1-2 Tbsp butter	1-2 Tbsp butter
yogurt (optional)	yogurt (optional)

A Proper Tea Party

Michael Lindfield came to the pantry, looking for tea. I said that the tea was kept in the shed; only essential everyday items like eggs, milk and toilet paper were kept in the pantry. He drew himself up. "To an Englishman," he said, "tea is far more essential than toilet paper."

As traditional as the tea itself are the various cakes and sweets that accompany it. Here we have the full array, taken from recipe files of some of the best bakers in the community.

Walnut Tarts

1. Let cream cheese and butter soften at room temperature, then mix together.
2. Stir in flour.
3. Chill dough for about one hour.
4. Shape into small balls; place in ungreased muffin tins and press dough into bottom and sides.
5. Prepare filling: beat together sugar, butter, vanilla and salt. Add egg and mix thoroughly.
6. Divide nuts in half. Sprinkle one half into bottoms of pastry cups; put a spoonful of filling in each cup; top with remaining nuts. Don't worry if it looks as though there isn't much filling in the tart. The filling expands as it bakes.
7. Bake at 170°C/Gas Mark 3/325°F for 25 minutes or until filling is set.
8. Allow to cool before removing from pans.

metric/imperial	american
Dough	Dough
85g/3oz cream cheese	6 Tbsp (3oz) cream cheese
110g/4oz butter or margarine	½ cup butter or margarine
130g/4½oz flour	1 cup flour
Filling	Filling
140g/5oz brown sugar	¾ cup brown sugar
1 Tbsp soft butter	1 Tbsp soft butter
½ tsp vanilla	½ tsp vanilla
pinch of salt	pinch of salt
1 egg, beaten	1 egg, beaten
70g/2½oz walnuts, hazelnuts or pecans, coarsely cut	⅔ cup walnuts, hazelnuts or pecans, coarsely cut

Scottish Shortbread

1. Preheat oven to 150°C/Gas Mark 1½/300°F
2. Have butter at room temperature. Rub butter, sugar and flour together till it can be pressed into a ball.
3. On a board flatten the ball of dough to about 1.5cm (½in) thick. Cut into triangles or rectangles. Prick with a fork. Place on a baking tin and sprinkle with sugar.
4. Bake for 45 minutes, or until just beginning to turn golden around the edges.

metric/imperial	american
340g/12oz flour	2½ cups flour
225g/8oz butter (no substitutes)	1 cup butter (no substitutes)
110g/4oz sugar	½ cup sugar

Date Wheels

1. Sift together flour, salt and soda. Set aside.
2. Cream together butter, sugar and egg until completely smooth. Add dry ingredients and mix well.
3. Chill dough thoroughly.
4. Cut dates into pieces. Cook dates in a saucepan with water and lemon juice, just until ingredients are soft and well mushed together.
5. Let date mixture get completely cold.
6. Roll dough out into a large rectangle about 1cm(¼in) thick.
7. Spread date filling on the dough almost, but not quite, to the edge.
8. Roll up like a Swiss roll (jelly roll).
9. Wrap in grease-proof (waxed) paper and chill overnight, or freeze for later use.
10. When ready to bake, preheat oven to 180°C/Gas Mark4/350°F.
11. Slice wheels 1cm(¼in) thick.
12. Bake on greased baking sheets for about 8 minutes, or until lightly browned.

metric/imperial	american
Dough	Dough
255g/9oz flour	2 cups flour
¼ tsp salt	¼ tsp salt
½ tsp bicarbonate of soda	½ tsp baking soda
110g/4oz butter or margarine	½ cup butter or margarine
270g/9½oz soft brown sugar	1½ cups light brown sugar
1 egg, beaten	1 egg, beaten
Filling	Filling
225g/8oz pitted dates	1¼ cups pitted dates, packed tightly
110ml/4floz water	½ cup water
1 tsp lemon juice	1 tsp lemon juice

Fairy Cakes

1. Preheat oven to 220°C/Gas Mark 7/425°F.
2. Beat margarine and sugar together until smooth. Add eggs and mix thoroughly.
3. Sift together dry ingredients. Add dry ingredients and milk to batter. Beat well.
4. Spoon into paper cases and bake for 15-20 minutes, or until golden.

metric/imperial	american
110g/4oz margarine	½ cup margarine
110g/4oz caster sugar	⅔ cup sugar
2 eggs	2 eggs
170g/6oz plain flour	1½ cups flour
1½ tsp baking powder	2 tsp baking powder
¼ tsp salt	¼ tsp salt
2 Tbsp milk	2½ Tbsp milk
15 cake cases	15 muffin papers

Butterscotch Biscuits

1. Sift together flour, soda, salt, cinnamon, cloves and nutmeg. Set aside.
2. Cream together butter and sugars until smooth. Add egg and mix well.
3. Thoroughly mix in dry ingredients.
4. Stir in chopped nuts.
5. Make dough into a roll and wrap in grease-proof (waxed) paper. Chill overnight.
6. Slice, and bake on greased baking sheet at 180°C/ Gas Mark 4/350°F for 10 minutes.

metric/imperial	american
570g/1lb 4oz flour	4½ cups flour
¾ tsp bicarbonate of soda	1 tsp baking soda
¾ tsp salt	1 tsp salt
¾ tsp cinnamon	1 tsp cinnamon
½ tsp cloves	½ tsp cloves
½ tsp nutmeg	½ tsp nutmeg
340g/12oz butter or margarine	1½ cups butter or margarine
185g/6½ oz soft brown sugar	1 cup light brown sugar
185g/6½ oz white sugar	1 cup white sugar
3 eggs, well beaten	3 eggs, well-beaten
130g/4½oz chopped walnuts or hazelnuts	1 cup chopped walnuts

Flap Jacks

1. Preheat oven to 170°C/Gas Mark 3/335°F.
2. Mix coconut and oats together; set aside.
3. Gently melt margarine, sugar, syrup, treacle and salt together. If using metric or imperial measure, the saucepan can be put directly on the scale and quantities weighed in it, to avoid a treacle-syrup mess.
4. Add oats and coconut to margarine mixture; combine thoroughly.
5. Press into a greased 20cm(8in) square baking tin. Sprinkle a little more coconut and oats on top.
6. Bake for 30-35 minutes.
7. Remove from oven and cut into pieces immediately, but leave in tin until absolutely cold.

metric/imperial	american
60g/2oz coconut	⅔ cup coconut
170g/6oz porridge oats	1¾ cups porridge oats
110g/4oz margarine	½ cup margarine
60g/2oz sugar	⅓ cup sugar
85g/3oz golden syrup	¼ cup golden syrup
85g/3oz treacle	¼ cup treacle or light molasses
½ tsp salt	½ tsp salt

Chocolate Chip Oat Cookies

1. Preheat oven to 210°C/Gas Mark 6/400°F.
2. Grease a flat baking sheet.
3. Beat butter, sugar and vanilla until smooth and fluffy; mix in the egg.
4. Sift together flour, salt, baking powder and soda; stir into butter-sugar mixture.
5. Add oats and mix thoroughly.
6. Stir in chocolate chips and nuts.
7. Drop by spoonfuls onto baking sheet.
8. Bake for 10 minutes, or until lightly browned.

metric/imperial	american
225g/8oz butter or margarine	1 cup butter or margarine
185g/6½ oz sugar	1 cup sugar
½ tsp vanilla	1 tsp vanilla
1 egg	1 egg
255g/9oz flour	2 cups flour
¾ tsp salt	1 tsp salt
¾ tsp baking powder	1 tsp baking powder
¾ tsp bicarbonate of soda	1 tsp baking soda
200g/7oz porridge oats	2 cups oats
340g/12oz chocolate chips or plain chocolate, chopped small	2 cups chocolate chips
60g/2oz chopped hazelnuts	½ cup chopped nuts

Kiftens

1. Beat butter, sugar and vanilla together until fluffy.
2. Put almonds through fine grinder.
3. Alternate adding almonds and flour to butter-sugar mixture. Mix thoroughly.
4. Form little crescents and place on ungreased baking tin.
5. Bake at 180°C/Gas Mark 4/350°F for 15-20 minutes, or until lightly browned.
6. While still warm, roll in icing (powdered) sugar.

metric/imperial	american
400g/14oz butter	1¾ cups butter
185g/6½oz sugar	1 cup sugar
1 tsp vanilla	1 tsp vanilla
140g/5oz shelled almonds	1 cup shelled almonds
510g/18oz flour	4 cups flour
110g/4oz icing sugar	1 cup powdered sugar

Carob Nut Brownies

1. Preheat oven to 180°C/Gas Mark 4/350°F.
2. Grease a 20cm(8in) square baking tin.
3. Beat butter, honey and sugar together until smooth.
4. Stir in beaten egg.
5. Sift dry ingredients together, add to batter and mix thoroughly.
6. Add vanilla and chopped nuts.
7. Spoon into baking tin and bake for 30-35 minutes, or until a fork inserted comes out clean.
8. Cut into squares when cool.

metric/imperial	american
110g/4oz butter or margarine	*½ cup butter or margarine*
110g/4oz honey	*⅓ cup honey*
60g/2oz brown sugar	*⅓ cup brown sugar*
1 egg	*1 egg*
85g/3oz flour	*⅔ cup flour*
60g/2oz carob powder	*½ cup carob powder*
¾ tsp baking powder	*1 tsp baking powder*
½ tsp salt	*½ tsp salt*
½ tsp vanilla	*1 tsp vanilla*
130g/4½oz chopped walnuts, cashews or a mixture of the two	*1 cup chopped walnuts, cashews or a mixture of the two*

Coconut Pyramids

1. Preheat oven to 170°C/Gas Mark 3/325°F.
2. Mix coconut, sugar and essence together.
3. Beat egg white until stiff, then fold into coconut mixture.
4. Make tiny pyramids, then lay on a sheet of rice paper on an ungreased tin.
5. Bake for 15-20 minutes, or until browned. Cool on wire tray. Remove from rice paper. The rice paper, which is edible, will stick to the bottoms of the pyramids.
6. Melt chocolate in double saucepan, or in a glass bowl placed over boiling water. Dip base of each pyramid in chocolate. Set on wire tray to dry.

metric/imperial	american
1 large egg white	*1 large egg white*
85g/3oz shredded coconut	*1 cup shredded coconut*
85g/3oz castor sugar	*½ cup white sugar*
½ tsp almond or vanilla essence	*½ tsp almond or vanilla essence*
rice paper	*rice paper*
85g/3oz plain chocolate	*3 squares semi-sweet cooking chocolate*

Ginger Cake

1. Preheat oven to 160°C/Gas Mark 2/315°F.
2. Line a 18cm(7in) square baking tin with grease-proof (waxed) paper, after first rubbing it with margarine.
3. Melt margarine, sugar and syrup together in a saucepan.
4. Sift dry ingredients together, then add margarine-sugar mixture and mix thoroughly.
5. Beat egg and milk together, then stir into batter.
6. Pour batter into baking tin. Bake for 1½ hours, or until a fork inserted comes out clean.
7. Let cake cool, then cut into squares.

metric/imperial	american
110g/4oz margarine	½ cup margarine
110g/4oz soft brown sugar	⅔ cup light brown sugar
110g/4oz golden syrup	⅓ cup golden syrup or corn syrup
200g/7oz plain flour	1¾ cups flour
½ tsp salt	½ tsp salt
3 tsp ginger (or more, if you like a strong ginger taste)	4 tsp ginger (or more, if you like a strong ginger taste)
1 tsp bicarbonate of soda	1¼ tsp baking soda
1 egg	1 egg
140ml/5floz milk	½ cup milk

Oatcakes

With brie and fruit, a complete snack.

1. Pour boiling water over currants. Set aside.
2. Preheat oven to 180°C/Gas Mark 4/350°F.
3. Rub a baking tin with butter.
4. Mix dry ingredients together, then add oil and mix thoroughly.
5. Drain currants, saving the liquid. Add currants to dough.
6. Add enough water so that ingredients hold together in a firm dough.
7. On a floured surface, roll dough out and cut into small rounds, 5cm(2in) in diameter.
8. Place on baking tin; bake for 15 minutes, or until cakes' are beginning to brown.

metric/imperial	american
85g/3oz currants (optional)	⅔ cup currants (optional)
190/7oz porridge oats	2 cups rolled oats
130g/4½oz oatmeal	1 cup oat flour
130g/4½oz soft wholemeal flour	1 cup whole wheat pastry flour
1 tsp salt	1 tsp salt
4 Tbsp oil	⅓ cup oil
110ml/4floz water or liquid from soaking currants	½ cup water or liquid from soaking currants

Currant Scones

Serve with whipped cream, butter and jam.

1. Preheat oven to 220°C/Gas Mark 7/425°F.
2. Pour enough boiling water over currants to cover them. Set aside.
3. Sift dry ingredients together.
4. Work butter into dry ingredients with fingers until the mixture resembles oats.
5. Drain water from currants and add them to the dough.
6. Add just enough milk so that dough can hold together when pressed into a ball.
7. On a floured surface pat dough out to about 2cm(¾in) thick. Cut fancy shapes or simple 5cm(2in) diameter circles.
8. Brush tops with milk and bake on an ungreased baking tin for 10-20 minutes, or until golden on top.
9. Serve immediately, wrapped in a cloth.

Variations

For cheese scones, omit currants and add 110g/4oz/1 cup grated cheddar cheese instead. Brush tops of scones with beaten egg, then sprinkle with more grated cheese.
For plain scones, omit currants.

metric/imperial	american
40g/1½oz currants	*½ cup currants*
280g/10oz flour	*2½ cups flour*
¾ tsp salt	*¾ tsp salt*
½ tsp bicarbonate of soda	*½ tsp baking soda*
¾ tsp baking powder	*1 tsp baking powder*
85g/3oz butter or margarine	*6 Tbsp butter or margarine*
140ml/5floz (approximately) sour milk, buttermilk or kefir	*⅔ cup (approximately) sour milk, buttermilk or kefir*

Cheese Straws

1. Sift together dry ingredients. Cut in shortening and margarine, then add remaining ingredients and mix thoroughly.
2. Roll out and cut in straws 1cm(~in) wide.
3. Bake at 240°C/Gas Mark 9/475°F for 7-10 minutes, or until browned.

metric/imperial	american
225g/8oz flour	*2 cups flour*
dash cayenne	*dash cayenne*
½ tsp salt	*½ tsp salt*
½ tsp mustard powder	*½ tsp mustard powder*
60g/2oz shortening	*¼ cup shortening*
85g/3oz margarine	*6 Tbsp margarine*
110g/4oz cheddar cheese, grated	*1 cup grated cheddar cheese*
170g/6oz parmesan cheese, grated	*1¾ cups grated parmesan cheese*
1 egg	*1 egg*

Desserts

All festivals, truly conceived and manifested, are necessary because in their own fashion they are part of the great rituals of life. They are periods when people come together in blending to create and release into the world the energies of upliftment and effervescence, of laughter, song and dance.

—*David Spangler, Festivals in the New Age.*

Desserts are a celebration. Birthdays, weddings, solstices, equinoxes, beginnings and endings all deserve special observances. In celebrating through food, we also celebrate our connection with the earth. What are the foods we eat at special times? Something as simple as the first raspberries of the season, served with cream, can be an elegant dessert. Or a pineapple, ripe and sweet, cut into chunks and served in its own shell. Or melon halves with the seed scooped out, then soured cream and blackberries piled into the centre. Unusual and different cheeses; each fruit as it comes into season.

Then there are the all-out extravagances, the real splurges, using ingredients we wouldn't normally use in our day-to-day lives. Most of the recipes in this section fall into that category. Special ingredients, extra time spent, elaborate decoration, uncommon tastes; in these ways we recognise and celebrate the unforgettable events in our lives.

Isla's Cake

A truly unforgettable chocolate cake, created for Isla's blessing when she was a baby.

1. Preheat oven to 180°C/Gas Mark 4/350°F.
2. Rub a 23cm(9in) deep, removable-bottom baking tin with butter, then dust with flour. Set aside.
3. Mix sugar, eggs and oil together until smooth.
4. Sift dry ingredients together, then add to batter and mix well.
5. Add hot water and mix it in, then milk, and mix thoroughly.
6. Add vanilla and walnuts.
7. For filling, mix sugar and cream cheese until smooth; blend in egg and vanilla; finally, add coconut and chocolate chips.
8. Pour half the cake batter into baking tin.
9. Spread filling evenly over batter (as filling is quite thick, this will need to be done with your fingers or with spoons).
10. Carefully pour other half of cake batter over filling.
11. Bake for 70 minutes, or until done (when a fork inserted in top part of cake comes out clean).
12. Remove from oven and let cake remain in baking tin until cool, as the filling is very soft and must be completely cool to become solid. This will take several hours.
13. Carefully remove cake from tin.
14. Ice cake on top and sides with whipped cream.

metric/imperial	american
Cake batter	Cake batter
390g/13oz sugar	2 cups sugar
225ml/8floz oil	1 cup oil
2 eggs	2 eggs
85g/3oz unsweetened cocoa powder	¾ cup unsweetened cocoa powder
400g/14oz flour	3 cups flour
1 tsp bicarbonate of soda	1 tsp baking soda
225ml/8floz hot water	1 cup hot water
225ml/8floz sour milk	1 cup sour milk
1 tsp vanilla	1 tsp vanilla
60g/2oz chopped walnuts	½ cup chopped walnuts
Filling	Filling
30g/1oz sugar	¾ cup sugar
225g/8oz cream cheese	8oz cream cheese
1 egg	1 egg
½ tsp vanilla	½ tsp vanilla
45g/1½oz shredded coconut	½ cup shredded coconut
225g/8oz semisweet chocolate chips or plain chocolate, chopped small	1 cup chocolate chips
Icing	Icing
⅓ litre/½ pint whipping cream, whipped	1½ cups whipping cream, whipped

Birthday Cake

1. Pour boiling water over butter, oats and honey. Cover for 20 minutes.
2. Preheat oven to 180°C/Gas Mark 4/350°F.
3. Rub a 33 x 23 x 5cm (13 x 9 x 2in) baking tin with butter; then using a tea strainer dust with flour.
4. Sift dry ingredients together and set aside.
5. Stir oats mixture until thoroughly blended, then mix in beaten eggs.
6. Add dry ingredients and mix well.
7. Pour into baking tin. Bake for 45 minutes, or until a fork inserted comes out clean.
8. Mix topping ingredients together.
9. If the baking tin is also appropriate for serving, topping can be spread on warm cake, browned under grill (broiler), then left to cool until serving time.
10. If cake is to be removed to a separate serving platter, choose one that can withstand the heat of the grill. Allow cake to cool first, then remove to platter. Spread cake. with topping and quickly brown under grill.

metric/imperial	american
280ml/10floz boiling water	*1¼ cups boiling water*
110g/4oz butter or margarine	*½ cup butter or margarine*
100g/3½oz rolled oats	*1 cup oatmeal*
170g/6oz honey	*½ cup honey*
185g/6½oz demerara sugar	*1 cup light brown sugar*
185g/6½oz soft wholemeal flour	*1½ cups whole wheat pastry flour*
¾ tsp bicarbonate of soda	*1 tsp baking soda*
1 tsp cinnamon	*1 tsp cinnamon*
¼ tsp salt	*¼ tsp salt*
2 eggs	*2 eggs*

Topping

Topping

85g/3oz butter, melted	*6 Tbsp butter, melted*
85g/3oz demerara sugar	*½ cup light brown sugar*
85g/3oz shredded coconut	*1 cup shredded coconut*
130g/4½oz chopped walnuts or hazelnuts	*1 cup chopped walnuts*
5 Tbsp cream or evaporated milk	*6 Tbsp cream or evaporated milk*

Shortcrust Pastry

1. Mix flour and salt.
2. Blend butter and shortening together thoroughly.
3. Cut butter-shortening mixture into flour, using a pastry blender or fingers until mixture resembles rolled oats.
4. Mix in ice water with a fork, one Tbsp at a time, using just enough water for dough to be gathered up in a ball.
5. If filling and crust are to be baked together, dough is now ready to be used. For a prebaked pastry shell, continue with steps 6 to 9.
6. Roll dough out; fit into baking dish; trim edges. Prick bottom and sides with a fork.
7. Place in refrigerator for one hour.
8. Preheat oven to 230°C/Gas Mark 8/450°F.
9. Remove crust from refrigerator and bake immediately for 10 – 12 minutes or until golden brown.

Suggestions

Shortcrust pastry can be mixed in advance, and left in the refrigerator for up to one week. For ease in handling, it should be removed from refrigerator one hour before rolling out. Margarine, butter and vegetable shortening can be used interchangeably although, for the beginner, margarine or vegetable shortening is easier to work with. After you are comfortable with mixing and rolling dough, use half butter for added flavour. The amount of salt needed will vary according to the type of shortening used. Handle the dough as little as possible. Mix it and roll it out quickly. Don't despair if your first crust is a bit odd. Experience brings better results.

metric/imperial	american
250g/8oz flour	2 cups flour
¾ tsp salt	1 tsp salt
60g/2oz butter	⅓ cup butter
60g/2oz vegetable shortening	⅔ cup vegetable shortening
5-6 Tbsp ice water	5-6 Tbsp ice water
Makes one 20cm(8in) double-crust pie, or two single-crust pies	Makes one 8in double-crust pie, or two single-crust pies.

Swede Pie

The usual response to this pie is astonishment that the humble swede could taste so good. One person called it 'Swede Surprise'.

Crust
1. Preheat oven to 220°C/Gas Mark 7/425°F.
2. Mix dry ingredients together.
3. Cut in butter until well blended.
4. Mix oil in with a fork.
5. Add as much water as needed to hold pastry together.
6. Press into 23cm(9in) round pie dish.
7. Bake for 10 minutes or until brown.
8. Allow pastry to cool before filling.

Filling
1. Wash, peel and chop swedes. Cook in small amount of boiling water until soft. Drain and save cooking water.
2. Heat milk and cooking water to just under boiling point.
3. Put swedes, cornflour, sugar, salt, cinnamon, nutmeg, cooking water, milk and lemon balm in blender. Blend until smooth.
4. Cook mixture in top of double saucepan, or in a bowl over boiling water, until it thickens. Cover and continue to cook another 10 minutes.
5. Separate eggs. Set whites aside. Beat egg yolks.
6. Add a few spoonfuls of swede mixture to egg yolks.
7. Return egg yolk mixture to saucepan and continue cooking for 2 minutes.
8. Remove from heat and allow to cool.
9. When mixture has cooled, beat egg whites until stiff.
10. Gently fold egg whites into swede mixture. Pour into baked crust.
11. Refrigerate for at least two hours.
12. Before serving, whip cream and spread over top of pie.

metric/imperial	american
Crust	Crust
40g/1½oz rolled oats	½ cup oatmeal
55g/2oz wholemeal flour	½ cup whole wheat pastry flour
30g/1oz freshly ground walnuts, or any other nut or seed	¼ cup ground walnuts, or any other nut or seed
1½ Tbsp demerara sugar	2 Tbsp light brown sugar
½ tsp cinnamon	½ tsp cinnamon
½ tsp salt	½ tsp salt
55g/2oz butter	4 Tbsp butter
1½ Tbsp oil	2 Tbsp oil
2 Tbsp water	2 Tbsp water

Filling	Filling
225g/8oz swede (weighed after peeling)	1 medium swede (rutabaga): 1¼ cups when
140ml/5floz cooking water	chopped and cooked
140ml/5floz milk	½ cup cooking water
2 Tbsp cornflour	½ cup milk
85g/3oz demerara sugar	2 Tbsp cornstarch
¼ tsp salt	½ cup light brown sugar
1 tsp cinnamon	¼ tsp salt
1 tsp nutmeg	1 tsp cinnamon
1 tsp fresh chopped lemon balm (if available)	1 tsp nutmeg
3 eggs	1 tsp fresh chopped lemon balm (if available)
140ml/5floz whipping cream	3 eggs
	1 cup whipping cream

Variations

In place of swedes use another vegetable, such as pumpkin, squash or parsnips. This recipe was originally made with turnips and was a resounding success, although we decided later that it tasted a bit too 'turnippy'.

Fresh Berry Pie

1. Wash and drain the berries.
2. Mash half the berries.
3. Mix cornflour, sugar and salt in a medium-sized saucepan.
4. Add mashed berries to cornflour mixture and cook until mixture becomes thick and clear.
5. Place remaining unmashed berries in the baked pie shell.
6. Pour hot berry mixture over fresh berries.
7. Cool. Refrigerate for at least one hour.
8. Top with whipped cream.

metric/imperial	american
One single-crust pie shell, prebaked (see recipe for Shortcrust Pastry)	One single-crust pie shell, prebaked (see recipe for Shortcrust Pastry)
500g/18oz fresh blackberries, strawberries or raspberries	4 cups fresh blackberries, strawberries or raspberries
3 Tbsp cornflour	3 Tbsp cornstarch
170g/6oz sugar or 340g/12oz mild honey	1 cup sugar or mild honey
¼ tsp salt	¼ tsp salt
140ml/5floz whipping cream	1 cup whipping cream

Homemade Apple Pie

1. Preheat oven to 180°C/Gas Mark 4/350°F.
2. Wash and core apples; slice thin.
3. Cut butter into small pieces. Mix apples, butter, flour, sugar, lemon juice and spices; stir until well mixed. Set this mixture aside while preparing the pastry.
4. Divide short crust pastry in half. Roll out half and fit into a large, round, glass pie dish (23cm/9in).
5. Taste the apple mixture and add more honey, lemon or spices if needed (apples differ greatly in flavour), then put apples into pie dish.
6. Roll out other half of pastry and cut strips about 2cm(¾in) wide
7. Lay these strips of dough across dish to make a lattice top (as in weaving).
8. Turn up pastry hanging over edge of pan, thus forming a ridge of dough around pan, blending all the ends of the lattice. Flute the edge around the pan.
9. Prepare an egg wash by beating an egg with 1 Tbsp water or milk, then brush dough with it. (Leftover egg can be used in other cooking.)
10. Bake pie for one hour, or until crust is golden brown and apples are tender when pierced.

Serving Suggestions

Serve warm with whipped cream, vanilla ice cream or cheddar cheese.
This pie is wholesome and filling: the perfect complement to a light meal
or brunch, practically a meal in itself when served for tea.

Variation
Add walnuts, sunflower seeds or any nut or seed to the apple mixture.

metric/imperial	american
Short crust Pastry for one double-crust pie, made with 84% wholemeal flour	Short crust Pastry for one double-crust pie, made with whole wheat pastry flour
900g/2lb cooking apples	2lb cooking apples
2 Tbsp butter or margarine	2 Tbsp butter or margarine
2 Tbsp flour	2 Tbsp flour
3 Tbsp brown sugar or 2 Tbsp honey	3 Tbsp brown sugar or 2 Tbsp honey
juice of ½ lemon	juice of ½ lemon
1½ tsp cinnamon	1½ tsp cinnamon
½ tsp ground cloves	½ tsp ground cloves
⅛ tsp ground cardamom	⅛ tsp ground cardamon
1 egg	1 egg

Crème Caramel

1. Clean and dry thoroughly a 1 litre/2 pint/1 quart fancy baking mould. Set aside.
2. Preheat oven to 160°C/Gas Mark 2/325°F.
3. Slowly heat sugar in a heavy saucepan, stirring constantly, until sugar turns to syrup and becomes caramel-coloured.
4. Pour syrup into baking mould. Tilt mould around so that syrup covers as much of the surface as possible. Be careful, as the syrup is very hot. Set mould aside to cool.
5. Pour boiling water slowly and carefully into the hot caramel saucepan. (It will spit and steam, due to high temperature.) Stir water around, so that caramel won't stick. By doing this immediately the saucepan will be much easier to clean afterwards.
6. Beat eggs. Set aside.
7. In a saucepan, heat milk slightly. Remove from heat.
8. Add sugar; mix until dissolved.
9. Add beaten eggs, vanilla and salt; blend thoroughly.
10. Pour into baking mould.
11. Set mould inside larger dish of hot water in oven. (It is a bit tricky getting the baking mould in and out of a pan of hot water in the oven, but it is definitely worth it for the result of better texture.)
12. Bake for 40–60 minutes, or until a knife inserted in the centre comes out clean.
13. Cool, then refrigerate for several hours.
14. Just before serving, unmould the dessert. First loosen the edges with a knife, then place serving platter upside down over mould. Holding mould and platter securely together, quickly flip the dessert over. Remove mould. The caramel will now be a sauce on top of the dessert.

Variations

Decorate with flowers. Serve with whipped cream on the side. Sprinkle with roasted cashews or almonds, chopped.

metric/imperial	american
55g/2oz sugar	8 Tbsp sugar
455ml/16floz milk	2 cups milk
4 eggs	4 eggs
6 Tbsp sugar or mild honey	½ cup sugar or mild honey
½ tsp vanilla	½ tsp vanilla
⅛ tsp salt	⅛ tsp salt

Cheesecake

1. Preheat oven to 160°C/Gas Mark 3/325°F.
2. Mix crumbs and butter together thoroughly, then press into a 20cm(8in) shallow baking tin, forming an even crust with your fingers.
3. Beat cream cheese until fluffy.
4. Blend in eggs.
5. Add honey, lemon juice, vanilla and salt; mix thoroughly.
6. Pour into pie crust and bake 25 to 30 minutes, or until set.
7. While pie is baking, mix topping ingredients together.
8. Pour topping over hot pie, and return to oven for an additional 10 minutes.
9. Cool, then chill for at least 8 hours.

metric/imperial

Crust
110g/4oz digestive biscuits, crushed fine
50g/2oz butter, melted

Filling
225g/8oz cream cheese
2 Tbsp mild, white honey
1 Tbsp lemon juice
½ tsp vanilla
⅛ tsp salt
2 eggs, beaten

Topping
¼ litre/½ pint soured cream
2 Tbsp honey
½ tsp vanilla

american

Crust
¼ cups graham cracker crumbs
¼ cup butter, melted

Filling
1 cup (8oz) cream cheese
8 Tbsp mild, white honey
1 Tbsp lemon juice
½ tsp vanilla
⅛ tsp salt
2 eggs, beaten

Topping
1 cup sour cream
2 Tbsp honey
½ tsp vanilla

Chocolate Cream Pie

1. Combine cocoa powder, sugar, cornflour and salt in a glass bowl or in the top of a double saucepan.
2. Add milk and mix thoroughly.
3. Place over pan of boiling water. Cook for about 10 minutes, stirring constantly. When it thickens, cover and cook for 10 minutes more.
4. Remove from heat. When slightly cooled, add vanilla and orange rind.
5. Pour into prebaked pie shell.
6. Cool, then refrigerate for at least two hours.
7. Top with whipped cream before serving.

metric/imperial (8 servings)

One 20cm(8in) single-crust pie shell, prebaked
  (see recipe for ShortcrustPastry)
5 Tbsp unsweetened cocoa powder
125g/4½oz sugar
5 Tbsp cornflour
⅛ tsp salt
700ml/1¼pints milk
½ tsp vanilla
½ tsp grated orange rind (optional)
140ml/5floz whipping cream

american (8 servings)

One 8in single-crust pie shell, prebaked
  (see recipe for Shortcrust Pastry)
6 Tbsp unsweetened cocoa powder
¾ cup sugar
6 Tbsp cornstarch
⅛ tsp salt
3 cups milk
½ tsp vanilla
½ tsp grated orange rind (optional)
1 cup whipping cream

Banana Cream Pie

1. Combine cornflour (cornstarch), salt and milk in a glass bowl or in the top of a double saucepan. Mix thoroughly.
2. Place over pan of boiling water. When mixture begins to get warm, add honey.
3. Continue cooking, stirring constantly, for about 10 minutes, or until mixture begins to thicken. Cover and cook for another 10 minutes.
4. In a separate bowl, stir 8 Tbsp of the thickened mixture into one well-beaten egg. Return this mixture to saucepan and blend thoroughly.
5. Continue to cook for another two minutes, stirring constantly.
6. Remove from heat. Allow to cool slightly.
7. While mixture is cooling, peel and slice banana into pie shell.
8. Stir vanilla into thickened milk mixture.
9. Pour mixture over banana in pie shell.
10. Allow pie to cool, then refrigerate for at least two hours.
11. Top with whipped cream before serving.

Variation

For a coconut cream pie, omit banana and add 90g/3oz/1 cup freshly grated coconut to the thickened milk mixture just before pouring into pie shell.
Top with whipped cream.

metric/imperial (6–8 servings)	american (6–8 servings)
One 20cm(8in) single-crust pie shell, prebaked (see recipe for Short crust Pastry)	*One 8in single-crust pie shell, prebaked (see recipe for shortcrust Pastry)*
3 Tbsp cornflour	*3 Tbsp cornstarch*
⅛ tsp salt	*⅛ tsp salt*
½ litre/1 pint milk	*2 cups milk*
4 Tbsp mild honey	*¼ cup mild honey*
1 egg, well-beaten	*1 egg, well-beaten*
1 banana	*1 banana*
½ tsp vanilla	*½ tsp vanilla*
140/5floz whipping cream	*1 cup whipping cream*

Traditional English Sherry Trifle

Madeira Cake

The cake for the trifle must be baked 3–7 days ahead of time. The trifle is better if, after topping with custard, it is refrigerated for several hours.

1. Preheat oven to 170°C/Gas Mark 3/325°F.
2. Rub a 23 x 12 x 7cm (9 x 5 x 2½in) baking tin with butter, then dust with flour.
3. Sift together flour, baking powder and salt. Set aside.
4. Cream together the butter and sugar.
5. Add beaten eggs, then mix thoroughly.
6. Blend in flour mixture until smooth. Pour into baking tin.
7. Bake for 1¼ hours or until done. Remove from pan.
8. Set cake in a safe place and allow it to become stale (3–7 days).

Filling

1. Drain juice from tinned fruit.
2. Slice cake and spread pieces with jam. Sandwich it. Cut into smaller pieces and fit in bottom of a large bowl, preferably glass, or use three small bowls.
3. Spoon sherry over the cake, just to soak cake but not make it mushy.
4. Arrange fruit on cake with sliced bananas.

metric/imperial (20 servings)	american (20 servings)
Madeira Cake	*Madeira Cake*
225g/8oz plain flour	*1¾ cups white flour*
1 tsp baking powder	*1 tsp baking powder*
⅛ tsp salt	*⅛ tsp salt*
170g/6oz butter or margarine	*¾ cup butter or margarine*
170g/6oz sugar	*1 cup sugar*
3 eggs	*3 eggs*
Filling	*Filling*
85g/3oz red jam	*½ cup red jam*
400g/14oz tin sliced peaches, pineapples or strawberries	*14oz can sliced peaches, pineapples or strawberries*
2 bananas	*2 bananas*
340ml/12floz cream sherry (approximately)	*1½ cups cream sherry (approximately)*

Custard

1. Heat milk. (Do not allow to boil.)
2. Beat eggs vigorously for one minute.
3. Into the top of a double saucepan, or a glass bowl, pour the milk through a strainer (to remove any skin that may have formed on the surface).
4. Pour eggs through the strainer into the milk. Stir in sugar.
5. Place pan over boiling water. Be sure that the bottom of the pan holding the custard does not touch the boiling water, but is suspended over it.
6. Cook mixture until it begins to thicken and will coat the back of a wooden spoon (10-15 minutes).
7. Remove from heat and add vanilla.
8. Immerse custard pan in cold water to speed cooling time. Change water if necessary.
9. Stir custard occasionally as it is cooling. Custard will thicken somewhat as it cools.
10. When custard has cooled, pour over the trifle to form a smooth layer on top.
11. Refrigerate for several hours or overnight.

Topping

1. Whip cream and spread over custard.
2. Cut cherries in half. Decorate the top with almonds and cherries.

Variations

Use fresh fruit or berries in place of tinned.

The trifle can be made in a single day if you purchase a cake which is already stale.

Custard	Custard
1 litre/2 pints milk	*4 cups milk*
6 Tbsp sugar	*6 Tb sp sugar*
6 eggs	*6 eggs*
½ tsp vanilla	*½ tsp vanilla*
Topping	Topping
1.4 litre/½ pint whipping cream (more if you wish to be extravagant)	*1 cup whipping cream (more if you wish to be extravagant)*
60g/2oz glacé cherries	*½ cup candied cherries*
30g/1oz toasted almond flakes	*¼ cup toasted almond flakes*

Banana Date Nut Wedding Cake

Cake

1. Preheat oven to 170°C/Gas Mark 4/350°F.
2. Lightly oil and thoroughly flour a large sheet pan. (Or two pans, each 48 x 38 x 4cm [19 x 15 x 1½in].)
3. Break eggs into mixer bowl and begin whisking at moderate speed.
4. Meanwhile sift all dry ingredients together and set aside.
5. When eggs are whipped and frothy, pour oil in slowly and continue whipping.
6. When eggs and oil are well mixed, stop mixer and pour honey in. Reduce speed and whip more. (Chop dates and nuts in the meantime.)
7. When liquid is well mixed, reduce speed and gradually add flour and mashed bananas alternately. You may need to stop mixing occasionally, to scrape bottom of bowl.
8. When batter is well mixed, add walnuts and dates. Mix one or two minutes, then give whole mix one final whip at high speed.
9. Turn into baking pan.
10. Bake for about 40 minutes, or until golden brown. (Knife inserted will come out clean.)
11. Cool well in pan.
12. To remove cake from pan, loosen edges with a knife, then place another pan the same size on top of cake, and holding firmly the sides of the pans, flip cake over. Now bottom will be showing. Next, place the serving platter over the cake and repeat the flipping procedure. The cake will now be right side up.
13. Tuck strips of greaseproof paper (waxed paper) under the edges of the cake so that the serving platter will remain clean while cake is being iced.

Icing

1. Grate orange rind; then juice oranges. Set grated rind and juice aside.
2. In a mixer, whip butter.
3. Add honey and mix until well blended.
4. Sift in milk powder, add orange juice, grated rind and vanilla; mix thoroughly.
5. Ice cake when completely cool. Decorate with flowers.

metric/imperial	american
9 eggs, room temperature	9 eggs, room temperature
1 kg/2lb 4oz 84% flour or mixture of 84% and unbleached white	8 cups whole wheat pastry flour or mixture of whole wheat pastry and unbleached white
1 tsp salt	1 tsp salt
28g/1oz bicarbonate of soda or half bicarbonate of soda and half baking powder	5 tsp baking soda or half baking soda and half baking powder
1 tsp cinnamon	1 tsp cinnamon
½ tsp nutmeg	½ tsp nutmeg
¼ tsp ginger	¼ tsp ginger
½ tsp cloves	½ tsp cloves
400ml/14floz safflower oil	1¾ cups safflower oil
840g/1lb 14oz honey	2½ cups honey
1.68kg/3lb 12oz mashed bananas, weighed after peeling (approximately 20 bananas)	7½ cups mashed bananas (approximately 20 bananas)
455g/1lb finely chopped dates	3 cups finely chopped dates
455g/1lb walnuts, finely chopped	3½ cups finely chopped walnuts

<u>Icing</u>

6 oranges	6 oranges
900g/2lb butter or margarine	4 cups butter or margarine
1.4kg/3lb honey	4 cups honey
455g/1lb milk powder	4 cups milk powder
1 tsp vanilla	1 tsp vanilla
fresh flowers	fresh flowers

Makes 50 generous servings (1 large sheet cake)	Makes 50 generous servings (1 large sheet cake)

This is the perfect dessert for a hot summer's night. Should one of these ever come to Northern Scotland, we are prepared!

Crust
1. Preheat oven to 150°C/Gas Mark 2/300°F.
2. Mix dry ingredients together.
3. Add melted butter and mix thoroughly.
4. Into a 23cm(9in) deep pie dish press crust mixture evenly with fingers.
5. Bake for 15 minutes. Cool thoroughly before filling.

Filling
1. Soften cream cheese with a spoon, then whisk together with yogurt.
2. Sift milk powder in and mix thoroughly.
3. Add lemon rind, vanilla and mashed bananas; stir until blended.
4. Add honey and mix well.
5. Gently fold in other fresh fruit. If using small berries, leave them whole. Pineapple or other fruit must be chopped into small chunks.
6. Pour mixture into pie crust.
7. Vadan says: "My favourite part (other than eating it) is decorating it. I usually intersperse banana slices with berries around the edges and make a mandala with fresh mint leaves and perhaps a strawberry in the centre."
8. Thoroughly freeze pie (overnight).
9. When ready to serve, remove from freezer and allow to thaw for 30-45 minutes before cutting. (If you have a very cold freezer, allow more time for thawing.)

metric/imperial	american
Crust	**Crust**
125g/5oz granola digestive biscuits, crushed fine	*1½ cups honey graham crackers, crushed fine*
30g/1oz walnuts or cashews; finely chopped	*¼ cup walnuts or cashews, finely chopped*
1 tsp cinnamon	*1 tsp cinnamon*
dash of cloves	*dash of cloves*
dash of allspice	*dash of allspice*
85g/3oz melted butter	*6 Tbsp melted butter*
Filling	**Filling**
450g/1lb cream cheese	*2 cups cream cheese*
225ml/8floz yogurt	*1 cup yogurt*
50g/2oz milk powder	*½ cup milk powder*
grated rind of a lemon	*grated rind of a lemon*
½ tsp vanilla	*1 tsp vanilla*
2 bananas, mashed	*2 bananas, mashed*
honey to taste (about 2 Tbsp)	*honey to taste (about 2 Tbsp)*
140g/5oz fresh fruit (berries or pineapple are nice)	*1 cup fresh fruit (berries or pineapple are nice)*
½ banana, a few berries, mint leaves for decoration	*½ banana, a few berries, mint leaves for decoration*

Very Chocolate Cake

We dedicate this cake to David Spangler,
the world's greatest chocolate fan.

Cake Instructions

1. Preheat oven to 180°C/Gas Mark 4/350°F.
2. Rub two round cake pans with butter, then dust with flour.
3. Pour boiling water over chocolate and butter. Cover and let melt.
4. Add sugar and mix thoroughly.
5. Blend flour in lightly.
6. Mix sour milk and soda together, then add to batter.
7. Add eggs and vanilla; stir until batter is thoroughly blended.
8. Pour into baking pans.
9. Bake for 30 minutes or until done.
10. Let cake cool about 5 minutes, then remove from pan and let cool completely before icing.

Icing Instructions

1. In a saucepan, mix all ingredients together except vanilla.
2. Boil until soft ball forms when a small amount of icing is dropped in a dish of cold water.
3. Add vanilla
4. Allow icing to cool before applying.

metric/imperial	american
110g/4oz bitter chocolate grated or	4 squares bitter chocolate, grated or
2½oz cocoa powder	¾ cup cocoa powder
110g/4oz butter (or 220g/8oz, if cocoa is used)	¼ cup butter (or ½ cup, if cocoa is used)
¼ litre/½ pint boiling water	1 cup boiling water
370g/13oz sugar	2 cups sugar
255g/9oz flour	2 cups flour
7 Tbsp sour milk	½ cup sour milk
1¼ tsp bicarbonate of soda	1½ tsp baking soda
2 beaten eggs	2 beaten eggs
2 tsp vanilla	2 tsp vanilla

Icing

metric/imperial	american
270g/9½ oz sugar	1½ cups sugar
90g/3oz bitter chocolate or 7 Tbsp cocoa	3 squares bitter chocolate or 9 Tbsp cocoa
¼ litre/½ pint cream	1 cup cream
1 Tbsp butter	1 Tbsp butter
½ tsp vanilla	½ tsp vanilla

Cooked Pears

I enjoy ending an especially elaborate meal with two desserts.
Cooked pears are an ideal first dessert course, as they are light and they
clean the palate. The next dessert then seems to be all the more delicious.

1. Wash pears. Leave whole.
2. Put pears in pan and add just enough water to immerse them halfway.
3. Remove pears from water. Measure water.
4. Bring water to boil. Then carefully add pears.
5. Reduce heat and simmer until almost tender (about 10 minutes).
6. Add sugar or honey and continue simmering until pears can be easily pierced with a fork but are not mushy. Taste syrup and add more sweetener if needed.
7. Remove from heat and add vanilla.
8. Allow pears to cool slightly, then split in half. Serve each half in a bowl, cut side down, with some syrup spooned over.

Variations

Add cinnamon, cloves, nutmeg. Use other fruits, such as peaches
or apricots. If this is the only dessert being served, leave the pear
whole and serve one per person.

metric/imperial

One half, firm, unripe pear per person

For each ½ litre/1 pint of water use
4 Tbsp demerara sugar or honey and
¼ tsp vanilla

american

One half, firm, unripe pear per person

For each 2 cups of water use
¼ cup brown sugar or honey and
¼ tsp vanilla

Chocolate Leaves

1. Pick rose leaves; choose leaves that are smooth and of different sizes for variety.
2. Break into individual leaves; wash and dry each one.
3. Slowly melt chocolate in the top of a double saucepan or in a glass bowl over simmering water. Do not boil water.
4. When chocolate is melted, remove pan from heat and add a few drops of peppermint flavouring. Taste to see that the amount is right.
5. Hold rose leaf vein side up.
6. Apply a thin coat of chocolate to leaf, using the handle of a wooden spoon. Spread chocolate to the edges, but do not allow to overflow to other side.
7. Gently put leaves on grease-proof (waxed) paper. Allow to set for 20-60 minutes, or until the leaf can be pulled away from the chocolate. The time varies greatly with the temperature of the kitchen. If the kitchen is too warm, the leaves may need to go into the refrigerator for a few minutes. But for greatest ease in pulling leaf away, don't allow chocolate to become totally hard.
8. Separate the rose leaf from the chocolate leaf, carefully and quickly, before the heat of the hand warms the chocolate. If bits of the leaf stick, use the point of a small knife to loosen them.
9. Set finished product in a cool place until serving time.
10. Arrange leaves on a plate, patterned side up.
11. Serve as an after-dinner mint.

Variations

In place of peppermint flavouring, use a flavoured liqueur or grated orange rind.
Use leaves as decoration for another dessert.

metric/imperial	american
100g/3½oz chocolate	*3½oz chocolate*
few drops peppermint flavouring	*few drops peppermint flavouring*
Serves 8 people, 3 or 4 leaves each.	*Serves 8 people, 3 or 4 leaves each.*

Grateful thanks to all who have contributed to this Cookbook. To Stephen Clark, whose idea it was to publish the original edition. To Sandra Kramer who edited and to Sharon Quiring who painstakingly typed the original edition. To the Findhorn Foundation Community, which supported the creation of the original cookbook in practical as well as in joyful and creative ways. Special thanks to Eric Franciscus and to John Freed who both gave logistical as well as personal support to the development of the original edition.

Many thanks to the creative cooks who have contributed recipes: Loren Stewart, Vadan Baker, Mary Coulman, Richard Valeriano, Eric Franciscus, Bill Flink, Peter Caddy, Ludja Bolla, Pam O'Neill, Bob Knox, Frances Edwards, Callie Miller, Deborah Horner, Jeff Dienst, Shelley Drogin, Lynn Imperatore, Rennie Innis, Bessie Schadee, Debi DeMarco, Clara Bianca Erede, Catherine Williamson, and Sabrina Dearborn.

The creation of this revised edition was a joyful project in which Karin and Thierry Bogliolo, the publishers, hosted me in their home and plied me with fine chocolates whilst we all did our respective jobs in creating the new edition. Karin did the major work on this edition, scanning and editing the former edition, as well as being the chef who fed the three of us with ever more delightful menus each day. Thierry balanced the team with his down-to-earth publishing sense as well as his exquisite taste in wine and cheese.

As always, it has been a pleasure to work with the illustrator Sarah Zoutewelle-Morris, whose artistic ability is equally matched by her gentle and profound wisdom.

About the Author

Kay Lynne Sherman was a caterer and cooking teacher before her initial visit to the Findhorn Community. During that visit she had a profoundly opening experience whilst stirring a pot of split pea soup in the Cluny kitchen; shortly afterwards she made the decision to return to the community to live for several years.

At present, Kay Lynne lives and works as a psychologist in Seattle and in Ashland, Oregon. She loves to enjoy food with her family and friends and can be persuaded to cook for the occasional big event. The majority of her professional time, however, is spent helping people to find the recipe for living their lives.

To people everywhere who are performing the sacred task of preparing food for their loved ones, she sends her blessings.

About the Artist

Sarah Zoutewelle-Morris, an American artist living in Holland, spent 6 years in the Findhorn Conmunity. She has illustrated a number of books and her whimsical graphics and calligraphy are regularly published in several countries.

In Holland, she has been expanding her art to include work in hospitals and nursing hones, including the leading of creativity workshops and trainings for healthcare professionals and other groups.

The cookbook was a fun and rewarding collaborative project. She's not sure which she enjoyed more, doing the illustrations and calligraphy, or testing the recipes, ('The chocolate cream pie seems quite good, but perhaps I'd better have another slice just to make sure'). In any event, doing the artwork was the least dangerous in regards to her waistline.

About the Findhorn Community

The Findhorn Community was born in 1962, when Peter and Eileen Caddy and Dorothy Maclean came to the Findhorn Bay Caravan Park near the village of Findhorn, in the north east of Scotland. The garden they planted flourished with spectacular success, based on Eileen's inner guidance, Dorothy's contact with the intelligence of nature, and Peter's strong will and determination to follow the guidance. The garden attracted many people to visit, and later to live and work there.

Forty years later the community is a vibrant and growing village, exploring new ways of living to express spiritual and holistic values in everyday life. The community is an experiment, an educational centre and an aspiring ecological village, which includes people from all walks of life, families, businesses, interest groups, creative artists, charitable initiatives and healing professionals.

People are united by the desire to live, work and learn together, and to make a contribution towards a better world. The community welcomes thousands of visitors each year and hopes to provide inspiration and information to help people create their own sustainable lifestyles that reflect the divinity in all life.

For more information please visit www.findhorn.org or write to Findhorn Foundation, The Park, Findhorn, Forres IV36 3TZ, Scotland.

Index